To the Muckamuck strikers, for their long and inspiring fight to achieve union recognition in another virtually unorganized industry—restaurants.

An Account to Settle

The Story of the
United Bank Workers (SORWUC)

by The Bank Book Collective
Illustrations and Cover by Pat Davitt

Press Gang Publishers   Vancouver

Canadian Cataloguing in Publication Data

Main entry under title:
An Account to Settle

      ISBN 0-88974-012-7

      1. United Bank Workers
      2. Trade-unions—Bank employees—
British Columbia I. Ainsworth, Jackie, 1950-

HD6528.B262U54   331.88'11'3321   C79-091203-1

First printing: September, 1979

Published in Canada by the collective of:
Press Gang Publishers
603 Powell Street
Vancouver, B.C. V6A 1H2

Printed and bound by union labour

Contents

Preface

The Bank Book Collective is: Jackie Ainsworth, Sheree Butt, Charlotte Johnson, Helen Potrebenko, Denise Poupard, Jean Rands, Linda Read, Ulryke Weissgerber, and Dodie Zerr. We are all clerical workers except Denise who is now a scaler. Many people helped us with this book. We would especially like to thank: Melody Rudd, Penny Goldsmith, Mary Schendlinger for typing and typesetting; Honey Maser, Don Stewart, Bernadette Stringer, Linda Field for proofreading; Tony Williams for his research; Susan Margaret and Heather MacNeill for their criticisms and suggestions; Pat Barter, Jean Burgess, Denise Kouri, Lynette Polson for their help with writing; Liza Fry, Laurie McGuigan, Sarah Davidson for their help with editing; Billie Carroll, Anne Hoekema, Carmen Metcalfe, Pat Smith for production; the Euphoniously Feminist and Non-Performing Quintet for help in choosing chapter titles and songs, for their inspirational rewriting of many of the lyrics and for their music on the Gibsons picket line.

In some cases in this book we use a person's real name and in some cases we don't. When we introduce a person and give her surname, that is her real name. If a person is introduced with no surname, we have invented a fictitious name for her. Throughout this book we often refer to the Labour Code and the labour law. When we use those terms, we are usually referring to the federal Canada Labour Code. Bank workers are covered by the federal labour law, though most workers are covered by provincial labour laws. You can obtain a copy of the provincial labour laws by contacting the provincial Department of Labour. Labour Canada, which can give you copies of the federal Labour Code, also has regional offices. If you wish further information about SORWUC contact us at Ste. 1114-207 West Hastings Street, Vancouver B.C. V6B 1H7, 681-2811 or 684-2834.

The Bank Book Collective

All those jobs so unfulfilling
Will not be done by us unwilling
Need a whole new way of working
Organize, Organize.
— traditional folk melody

1   Victory Square

Shirley was a teller and a single parent. When she had to work overtime, she was late picking up her child at the day care centre. As the day care workers didn't get paid for overtime either, they weren't too pleased about this situation and pressured Shirley to be on time. So at 5:00 p.m. she walked out instead of filing cheques.

Jackie Ainsworth, a founding member of SORWUC (Service, Office and Retail Workers Union of Canada) is a ledgerkeeper at the Victory Square branch of the Canadian Imperial Bank of Commerce in downtown Vancouver. She describes that day in the summer of 1976:

As we were putting on our jackets at our lockers, the assistant accountant came and told us that she wanted the cheques filed and that none of us were to leave until they had been filed. It had been a long day, we had had no coffee break, and a couple of tellers were out on their balances. After everyone finally balanced, I was in no mood to start filing and neither was anyone else. Tired and furious, we took off our jackets and headed for the filing cabinets. All except Shirley, who said she'd had it for the day and was leaving. We watched her walk to the front of the branch and sign out in the time book. The assistant accountant ran over to her and seemed to be explaining while Shirley seemed to be arguing. The conversation went on for about five minutes, and then Shirley left. We didn't know if she had quit or had been fired or if they had worked something out.

The following day Shirley was at work and explained that she had been allowed to leave that night but could never do it again. If she had problems with day care arrangements, she had better work them out in some way that allowed her to work involuntary unpaid overtime whenever the bank's needs required it. All the tellers and ledgerkeepers discussed the matter at our wickets and desks. We decided to approach the accountant to say we would share Shirley's overtime so she could leave at 5:00 p.m. The accountant, who was a young and arrogant man and new to the branch, said that was very noble of us but if someone didn't meet the requirements of the job, they should quit. We decided to meet in the pub after work to discuss the matter as it seemed grossly unfair.

At Victory Square we regularly worked overtime. Some of us thought this was because the branch was short-staffed; others thought the tellers were incompetent. If one teller didn't balance, no one could go home until the difference was found. This put incredible pressure on the individual and caused tension among the employees.

With the exception of the head teller all the people on our side of the branch were invited to the meeting at the pub. (Tellers, ledgerkeepers and steno are on one side of the branch; the managers, accountant, loans officer and two secretaries on the other.) Six women attended and two others who supported the idea were unable to come. The first thing we discussed was the exclusion of the head teller. Although she was not a supervisor, the tellers thought of her as a sort of supervisor who might fink to management. The fact that the secretaries weren't invited wasn't even discussed. (In later months the head teller and one of the secretaries were to become active union members and the head teller was elected the first representative of the branch to the union executive.)

Overtime wasn't the only complaint we discussed. The tellers resented the arbitrary power of the supervisors. We were angry about what we saw as personal favouritism towards certain staff members and petty harassment of others. Supervisors had the power to recommend promotion and transfer based on their personal likes and dislikes with no regard to seniority. New tellers were not given adequate training and then were blamed by management and even their co-workers when they failed to balance. When annual cost of living increases were announced, we discovered that the new teller who had no previous banking experience was making more money than our head teller who had worked there for one and a half years.

The main purpose of our meeting was to discuss what we could do to make Regional Office aware of our dissatisfaction. The tellers suggested walking out en masse the following Friday during the peak time in the branch. The ledgers department argued against this action, saying the only result would be that everyone would get fired and replaced by women from the Regional Training Centre which was only three blocks away. There was discussion of a petition to the Regional Office. This idea was rejected on the grounds that it would just end up in someone's wastepaper basket after the names on it were noted. The idea of going to the branch manager was also rejected on the grounds that the manager had no power to act on complaints involving low wages, discrepancies in wages, short staffing and the lack of available training. These are all determined by Regional Office.

I raised the issue of union organizing. Everyone at the meeting thought a union was just what we needed; that a union in the banks would solve many of the problems. However, it seemed then to be a crazy, impossible idea.

The total assets of the Canadian chartered banks in 1976 were $119,944,425,000. There were 7,113 bank branches in Canada of which 836 were in B.C. They employed 130,111 people.

We were just six people in one branch in Vancouver. The bank was so big and powerful there seemed to be no way to make ourselves heard.

A union was a nice dream, but what could we do that was practical? The meeting ended after a couple of hours with everyone very discouraged.

SORWUC had already signed up a few members in banks as a result of leafletting downtown office buildings. When I started working at Victory Square, we in SORWUC had hoped that in a year or so we could get together an organizing committee in the banks. But this first meeting took place after I had been there barely three months.

The day Shirley walked out, I had called the SORWUC office. The next morning, a leaflet about overtime was handed to employees as we went to work by two SORWUC members who worked as volunteers in the union office. The leaflet said that the issue of overtime, overtime pay and the right to refuse to work overtime could be dealt with effectively only with a union contract. It gave the phone number of the SORWUC office and asked people to call for further information. The Toronto-Dominion Bank across the street was also leafletted so that it wouldn't be too conspicuous that we were singling out the Commerce Victory Square branch.

The leaflet resulted in a discussion among tellers about our wages and how disgustingly low they were. At the time (1976) the starting rate was about $600 a month in Vancouver while outside Vancouver it was as low as $525. There seemed to be no rational system for determining the annual merit increases beyond who liked you in the branch. We also talked about the lack of pay for overtime. (The banks had a special exemption from the law that workers must be paid for working overtime. By means of an arrangement with the Ministry of Finance, overtime in banks was "averaged". If one night everyone worked late and another night they were sent home early, the two were considered to cancel each other out, and no overtime was paid. The Banks were allowed to average overtime over a thirteen week period so that employees could be required to work overtime every day for several weeks without pay.)

The discussion continued over the next four or five weeks. Dodie Zerr, the current accounts ledgerkeeper, Karen, the head teller, and I became good friends, and committed to the idea of organizing a union in the banks. We got together almost every night after work. I told everyone about SORWUC; why and how it was formed. We talked about "good" and "bad" unions, about the laws that govern unions, how to apply for certification and, of course, who we should approach to join the union at the Victory Square branch. The three of us and Shirley went to a meeting of SORWUC Local 1 on July 22, 1976.

There were about thirty people at the meeting, mostly women. The meeting was in a member's house. The union office was in her basement and was staffed by volunteer labour — there were no paid officers. The office had a typewriter, SORWUC's first capital expense, purchased in January 1976, and a mimeograph machine which had been donated.

Most of the people at the meeting were not working in places where SORWUC had contracts, but were "members at large", committed to the idea of a working women's union. We discussed the appeal to the Unemployment Insurance Commission about a SORWUC member being cut off maternity benefits and denied regular benefits. The meeting decided to hold a mail vote of all members on whether or not to affiliate to the B.C. Federation of Women, an umbrella organization of women's groups. At that time, the union was a grass-roots, women-oriented union (and that's pretty much what we remain today). SORWUC's origins are in the Working Women's Association (WWA) which in 1971 and 1972 was active in supporting strikes of women in predominantly unorganized industries struggling to achieve union recognition. The WWA had done informational leafletting about UIC, equal pay, day care, job security, as well as the federal and provincial labour laws. Members of WWA were involved in union drives at Smitty's Pancake House, Pizza Patio, Denny's and the University of B.C. It was apparent that the existing unions were not prepared to undertake the kind of fight that would be required to organize unorganized industries. They saw banks, restaurants and offices as unorganizable.

The WWA had finally decided what was needed was a union whose main objective was to organize the unorganized. And so SORWUC was formed in October 1972. We didn't want a union run by highly-paid professional union leaders. So the constitution included: referendum election of all officers; referendum ballots for any dues increase; a limit on the length of time any member could hold a paid position in the union; and a provision that the salary for such a position would be no greater than the highest wage in a SORWUC contract. Locals of the union were given complete control of their own affairs and the right to secede from SORWUC upon majority vote of the local membership. The new union encouraged members in each workplace to write their own contract proposals and conduct their own negotiations for a union contract.

During a break in the meeting, one of the bank workers said that she had never attended a "women's liberation" meeting before.

The meeting heard reports on the workplaces which were organized by SORWUC — four day care centres, five social service units, one legal office, one student society office and a tuxedo rental store. All but two of these were in the public sector. Negotiating wage increases for public service employees is difficult. For instance, day care workers' contracts were negotiated with non-profit societies composed of parents, many of whom were single mothers working for equally low wages in offices or banks. In July 1976 SORWUC members were preparing to go on strike against a private sector employer, Mallabar Tuxedo Rentals Ltd.

The meeting decided to rent office space downtown, choosing the Dominion Building near Victory Square because of low rent and convenient location. We discussed the leafletting campaign that had been going on for several months. SORWUC leaflets were distributed at major office centres and banks in downtown Vancouver. The leaflets discussed wages and working conditions of clerical workers and stressed the need for unionization to overcome these inequities. That spring the union had held a series of noon hour information meetings at the downtown library.

Although the main branch of the Commerce had been leafletted and a few workers there joined SORWUC, we four Victory Square bank workers were the first to attend a meeting. At this July meeting Dodie, Karen and Shirley joined the union, and we were all authorized to sign up other bank workers.

The Canada Labour Code, which is the labour law covering banks and bank workers, would require the banks to recognize our union and negotiate with us once we were "certified". The Canada Labour Relations Board (CLRB) is the body appointed by the federal Cabinet to administer the Labour Code. The Board decides whether or not a union will be certified. When the union applies for certification, we have to say what "bargaining unit" we are applying for and demonstrate that we have a majority. The bargaining unit is all the people who will be covered by the union contract once it is signed, whether they are union members or not. Like porridge and chairs, bargaining units are supposed to be neither too hot nor too cold nor too large nor too small. The bigger the bargaining unit, the more bargaining power the union will have. However, in order to get certified, the union has to have the support of the majority of the bargaining unit and increasing the size of that unit could make that more difficult. The union can express an opinion about what the bargaining unit should be, but it is the Labour Relations Board that decides.

At this time there were several myths about a union in the banks, the most common of which was that the bargaining unit had to be "The Nation". This would mean that to organize a bank we would have to sign up a majority of all the employees of that bank across the country before we could be certified. This, of course, would make organizing impossible and contradict the labour law which states that bank workers in Canada have the right to join a union of their choice.

In 1959, the Canada Labour Relations Board had rejected an application for certification for a small bank branch in Kitimat, B.C. The Board ruled that this branch was not an appropriate bargaining unit, but went on to say: "This decision must not be taken as indicating that the Board agrees with the respondent's (bank's) contention that the appropriate unit must be a nation-wide unit of employees of the Bank. . . It may well be that units of some of the employees of a bank, grouped together territorially or on some other basis, will prove to be appropriate, rather than a nation-wide unit." For the next seventeen years this decision would be used by unions as well as the banks as evidence of the impossibility of organizing banks.

In spite of all this, we decided to go ahead and apply for certification for our branch, Victory Square. There was no other way to start the campaign. We then had to decide which jobs in our branch should be included in the bargaining unit, and which should be excluded because they were management rather than workers. We decided to try to include everyone except the manager, the assistant manager and the accountant. The final decision would be made by the Board.

We divided up the list of Victory Square employees and each of us took on the task of approaching a certain number of individuals. By the second week in August, nine out of twenty employees at Victory Square had joined the union. We were nervous about approaching people who we thought might tell management. Finally we decided to apply for certification on Monday, August 16 whether we had a majority or not. Applying for certification simply involves filling out a form provided by the CLRB and sending it to them for investigation. The information required on this form includes the name and address of the employer and the union, a description of the bargaining unit for which the union is applying, the total number of employees in the unit, and the number of union members. The Canada Labour Code states that a union may apply for certification with thirty-five per cent or more of the employees signed up. If the union's membership is more than thirty-five per cent but less than a majority, a vote is taken to determine the wishes of all employees. If more than fifty per cent join the union, no vote is necessary.

WORKERS IN THE MONEY MARKET (1973): WHERE ARE THE WOMEN? *				PERCENT BY SEX
TYPE OF WORK	No. of MEN	No. of WOMEN		
EXECUTIVE & MANAGERIAL	9,765 ♂			96.1% ♂
		397 ♀		3.9% ♀
SUPERVISORY	18,501 ♂			82.7% ♂
		7,711 ♀		17.3% ♀
CLERICAL & RELATED **	17,389 ♂			16.1% ♂
		90,483 ♀		83.9% ♀
MAINTENANCE & SERVICE	2,661 ♂			71.8% ♂
		1,045 ♀		28.2% ♀
SALESMEN & AGENTS	2,847 ♂			84.6% ♂
		520 ♀		15.4% ♀
TOTALS ♂ ♀	51,163	100,157	} 151,319 PEOPLE EMPLOYED	66.2% ♀

* Source: "Total Employed, Banks and Other Accepting Establishments, by Type of Work, and Sex", *Statistics Canada*, 72-603, October 1973 (latest available).

** 'Clerical and Related' is defined as follows: "This group includes occupations concerned with recording, transcribing, typing, composing correspondence, classifying and filing, organizing and recording data into accounts and quantitative records, paying and receiving money, operating office machines and electronic data processing equipment, performing other minor administrative and general clerical duties. Examples in this category are: Clerk, Typist, Stenographer, Secretary, Account Clerk, Audit Clerk, Bookkeeper, Payroll Clerk, Bank Cashier, Bank Teller, Annuity Record Clerk, Claims Calculator, Securities Clerk, Statistical Clerk, Office Machine Operator, Adjusters, etc."

That weekend we made a last-ditch effort to sign up a majority. Although it was recognized that "outsiders" would be less effective in signing people up than would employees of the branch, it was thought necessary to try to protect the union activists in the branch. SORWUC members who were not employees at Victory Square phoned or visited three of the people we were hesitant about. None of the three joined.

We had decided to apply with less than fifty per cent just to get the thing started. We thought that after we applied and were able to come out in the open and argue with people, we could convince others to join. Also, some of the employees wanted to apply for union certification just to show Head Office how upset we were. Even if we lost, at least our protest would be registered.

The application for certification went in when the doors of the Vancouver office of the CLRB opened on Monday, August 16. The usual procedure is that the CLRB notifies the employer by mail that such an application has been made. But we thought someone might have told management what was going on, so we decided to officially tell them ourselves. This was to prevent the bank from firing union activists on some pretext at a time when the bank could pretend it knew nothing of the union application. The Canada Labour Code makes it illegal to fire people for union activity but they can be fired for any other reason, or even no reason at all, as long as it's not for union activity.

At 10:00 a.m. Jean Rands, Local 1 Vice-President, and Melody Rudd, Provincial Secretary-Treasurer of the Association of University and College Employees (AUCE), a sister union, came to the branch and asked to see the manager. They were told the manager was on vacation and the assistant manager was in a meeting with a customer which would be quite a while and that he then had to leave for another appointment. Jean and Melody said they would wait.

The "customer" in to see the assistant manager was the regional general manager of the B.C./Yukon Region. He had arrived at the branch at 9:00 a.m. and we had all been individually introduced. He said he was making one of his "regular" branch visits although none of us had ever seen him before.

After Jean and Melody had waited a while, the assistant manager came out of his office to see them. Jean handed him a copy of the application with the CLRB "received" stamp on it and told him that SORWUC had applied for certification on behalf of the employees at the branch. The assistant manager nervously said he didn't know what to do or say, to which Melody replied, "I think congratulations are in order." Then Jean and Melody left.

There was little work done in the branch the rest of the day. The regional general manager left. The union people were very quiet. When asked about the application, we said we didn't know anything about it. The manager arrived at noon, having been called back from vacation.

SORWUC held a press conference at our union office (located across the street from Victory Square) to announce the application.

Our National President, Elizabeth Godley, described it to the press as a "historic application". By mid afternoon, there were TV cameras at the branch and reporters asking for the bank's comments. That afternoon and in the following days, we received phone calls and several telegrams at Victory Square from other bank employees congratulating us. A few data centre employees included notes of support and congratulations among the cheques that were sent to the branch each morning.

The same day as the application was filed, two women arrived from the Regional Office. We were told they had come to help us with our problem of short staffing. I recognized one of the women as Dorothy Hooper, the personnel officer at Regional Office who had interviewed and hired me. Others remembered Bonnie Wong from the Methods and Organization Department. She had spent some time in the branch doing an efficiency study for Regional Office — timing people's work and rearranging their desks. These two became the main leaders in the campaign against the union. They questioned individuals about their union involvement and organized anti-union meetings.

Mary, the steno, was at home sick after hurting her finger in the addressograph machine at work. One evening she received a call from Bonnie Wong. Wong said there had been a staff meeting at work that day, during which the union members in the branch had identified themselves and claimed Mary as one of them. Mary agreed that she had joined the union. There had been a staff meeting, but no one had claimed their union membership. Mary's admission was the first evidence the bank had that she had joined.

This phone call was followed by a visit the next day. Mary called me at the branch at 11:00 a.m. to say that Sharon, Mary's supervisor, and Bonnie Wong were on their way to visit her at home with a letter they wanted her to sign resigning from the union. Mary wanted another union member to be there when they arrived. I called the union office and it was decided that Jean would go to Mary's house. When Jean arrived, she and Mary decided it would be better for Jean to wait in the kitchen and take notes, while Mary argued and tried to get the letter from them. Since they were making this visit on company time, it seemed obvious they had the manager's permission. We were convinced they were violating the Labour Code where it says no employer or representative of the employer shall "seek, by intimidation, threat of dismissal or any other kind of threat, by the imposition of a pecuniary or other penalty or by any other means, to compel a person to refrain from becoming or cease to be a member, officer or representative of a trade union. . ."

We felt that by getting evidence together about their visit with Mary, we would have grounds to lay a complaint of unfair labour practice with the CLRB. The Board would then order the bank to stop harassing and intimidating employees, and let the bank know that no attention would be paid to letters extracted from employees in this way.

During the visit, Wong told Mary that because she was a union member she was "labelled". She said that if Mary tried to get a job in another bank or office her chances would be pretty poor. She said "Orientals are known as good workers. That is why the bank hires us and has treated us so well. We do not want to spoil it." She told Mary her objective was "to smash the union". She asked Mary to sign a letter of withdrawal from the union. She would not give Mary the actual letter although Mary kept trying to grab it from her.

At the end of the meeting, Jean confronted Sharon and Bonnie, saying that what they had done was an unfair labour practice and that we intended to take the matter to the CLRB. Bonnie and Sharon arrived back at the branch, charging the union with "foul and dirty" tactics.

The harassment of Mary continued on a personal level until she withdrew her unfair labour practice complaint and eventually quit her job. Although we argued we still had grounds for complaint as a union, the case was never heard by the CLRB.

The anti-union employees went on to form a group called BIG — Bankers Independent Group — and started to get in touch with supervisors in other branches where the union was active.

Nicolia May found a book called "Organize"
And she understood every word to her suprise
So with an old sail and a novice crew
They made a great big wave on the ocean blue
— Nicolia by Holly Near

2   A Great Big Wave

While the banks were getting their anti-union act together, we were going crazy at the union office. Employees from branches all over B.C. were calling for information and many wanted to join. In the first six weeks after the Victory Square application, we applied for ten more branches. These branches were: Bank of Montreal at Edmonds and Kingsway, Cloverdale, Langley and Ganges; Commerce at Ocean Park, Port Hardy and Ganges; and the Bank of Nova Scotia at Simon Fraser University (SFU), Vancouver Heights and Haney. Karen, Dodie and Jackie from Victory Square, several Local 1 members, and Melody would go in pairs to meetings set up by branch employees and talk to them about the union, explaining why we had joined and why it was important for them to join with us to build a union strong enough to take on the banks.

Melody and Dodie went to Salt Spring Island and signed up a majority in all of the banks on the Gulf Islands (the two branches in Ganges). We talked by phone to employees of the Port Hardy branch and mailed applications to them. Most branches, however, were signed up at meetings in employees' homes. These meetings usually involved a majority of the employees in the branch. Sometimes supervisors were adamantly opposed to the union and sometimes they called the union meetings and were the first to join. The loans officers were the hardest to convince as they were usually men who expected to get promoted to branch manager some day.

The average size of a branch is approximately twelve people (including two management positions). Banks have an incredible hierarchical structure. In such a branch it would not be surprising to find four tellers (one a head teller), two ledger clerks, an assistant accountant (who supervises the teller and ledger departments), a secretary, a loans clerk, a loans officer, an accountant (who supervises the secretary, the loans clerk and the loans officer), and a manager.

At the organizing meetings we always spent a long time discussing who should be in the bargaining unit and who we wanted excluded. Again, it was all guess work since the Board would not only decide whether the branch was an appropriate unit, they would also rule on this whole inclusion/exclusion question. We could make some educated guesses. We and the banks would agree on excluding the manager and the accountant who generally acts as personnel manager in the branch. They both hire and fire employees and therefore should not be in the union. However, we suspected the banks would also want to exclude the branch secretary because of the supposedly confidential nature of her work, and the loans officers and management trainees as they supposedly performed management functions. The banks later made the expected arguments in regard to these positions; each bank also argued for the exlusion of all part-time employees.

In our first meetings it was difficult for us to separate the individual from the position. If the secretary was anti-union, branch employees would want the secretarial position excluded. Or if, by excluding the part-time employees, the union then had a majority, some people would want to exclude part-timers from the union! Secretaries and part-time workers were skilled and valuable employees who were often among the poorest paid and most in need of union protection. We ended up feeling very strongly about their inclusion.

Although as individuals the loans officers were mostly anti-union, this position was one to which women were generally denied access, and we wanted it to come under the seniority terms in a collective agreement. Assistant accountants performed supervisory functions and were sometimes seen as management, but in fact they mostly did their own work, and did not have the power to hire or fire employees. We were ambivalent about management trainees. In addition to doing our regular work, we had to train the trainees who were usually young men. We resented the fact that we could wait ten years for a promotion while they could be loans officers within a few months. While they were training for management, they were supposedly doing the same work as we were. We wanted those trainee positions to be subject to the seniority provisions in the contract so that clerical workers would have access to training programs. In larger branches, we agreed that assistant managers should be excluded, but we argued that loans officers, assistant accountants and management trainees should be included in the unit. It seemed that in terms of bargaining power, the more employees included in the unit the better. If it was necessary to take strike action, we didn't want the banks to be able to run a branch without the union people.

When people asked us to meet with their branch, we encouraged them to invite as many co-workers as possible. If someone was left out it could be used as an argument that the union was secretive and sneaky. On the other hand, sometimes when supervisors came, people were afraid to join the union or to speak up about the conditions in their branch. Our objective was that all the arguments for and against should be out in the open so people could make an informed decision.

The issues at these meetings were generally the same. Wages were always at the top of the list, seniority next, then deductions for cash shortages, vacations, sick leave, overtime, training management trainees, overcrowding, shortstaffing and others.

Some of the arguments against the union at these meetings were: you people are crazy, there's no way you can do this; banks are so powerful they run the government, how can you hope to win; we already have great benefits; we'll be ordered out on strike; I've already got enough people bossing me around; and others. We answered that the Labour Code specifically says bank workers can unionize; that a union of bank workers would be one of the biggest unions in the country; that we were organizing ourselves democratically; that no branch could strike unless members in that branch voted to strike; and that the only way to have any say in our working conditions was through the union. But the most effective answers came from branch employees who told us of injustices they had suffered or witnessed. They compared their pay to the wages of husbands and friends who were union members.

Our strategy at this time was to get as many applications as possible before the CLRB. We wanted to prove that Victory Square was not an isolated incident; that bank workers all over B.C. wanted a ruling on their right to have a union. Although it was best to apply with a majority of branch employees, we often applied with less. We needed as many applications as possible before the Board called the hearings.

After the first application, bank workers from all over B.C. joined the union. Among these were the employees of the Port McNeill branch of the Commerce. Denise Poupard, one of these employees, tells the story:

In July 1976, I was hired by the Commerce in Port McNeill (at the northern end of Vancouver Island). I was new to the village and unaware of the bank's reputation as a poor place to work. I was shocked when friends advised me to turn down the job and wait until something —anything else—turned up. They were right.

The branch was in rough shape that summer. There had been three complete turnovers in the teller line in six months. The two tellers had been given only one day's training on cash when they were hired and the next day were the only tellers at the branch. As the posting machine was broken, every day the accountant and the ledgerkeeper travelled forty-five kilometres to use the machine at the Commerce branch in Port Hardy. On the floor were boxes of filing that had never been done. Days were long, overtime "averaged out" (i.e. unpaid), balancing a miracle, and coffee breaks non-existent. I was lucky—a few months earlier when the branch had been "the only bank in town" and customers lined up outside every Friday, things had been even worse.

In August 1976, we heard about a Commerce branch in Vancouver joining a union. Within a week, we were given a half hour coffee break Tuesday through Thursday at 9 a.m. (We started work at 8:30.) Because our branch was so small, we went across the street to the restaurant for the break. It was there that somebody casually mentioned the union branch in Vancouver. The management trainee who was with us became quite upset and said anybody who joined a union would lose their job and that on his previous job, union dues were so high that he could hardly live on the few dollars that were left of his paycheque. While most of our group felt they could not risk losing their jobs, a couple of us argued with the trainee as we knew he was using fabricated anti-union scare tactics. But the threat of job loss, no matter how exaggerated, is a serious matter, so the subject was dropped.

By November we had become pretty sick of listening to ourselves complain. Day after day we spent our coffee breaks telling each other about the rotten pay; the supervisors who continually harassed and insulted us; the hours and the conditions. Finally one woman said: "I've got half a mind to join the union." The trainee, who had told management of our earlier discussion and tailed us to coffee ever since, was not there that day. Tired of our hopeless whining, I said: "Let's not just talk, let's do it." Nobody had to convince anybody else. One of us contacted a woman from the Commerce in Port Hardy which had joined the union shortly before. Some of those women came to Port McNeill for a clandestine meeting. It felt so good to realize that although each branch had unique conditions, we were all saying basically the same thing: underpaid, overworked, no security, no bargaining power, and mad enough to try to force a change.

Shortly after, we held another meeting among ourselves to reach a final decision. Advised to be wary of management finding out about our talk before a majority had joined and our union application was announced, we only discussed unionization with people we were sure of. We were probably angry enough to join any union but we joined SORWUC, impressed by what the Port Hardy women had told us about the union's philosophies. It was a lucky choice and a good one.

A few days after we announced our application for certification, our accountant told three members during coffee break that they would be asked to sign a paper saying that they had been coerced into joining the union. He was told in unprintable words what they thought of that idea. They stuck by their decision.

The biggest risk was taken by our steno, a single mother with three young children. In an isolated boom town where rent and food prices were based on loggers' union wages, her wage was so low that welfare was subsidizing her income. One of the richest corporations in Canada was not paying an employee enough for her and her family to survive! Embarrassed by public knowledge of the situation, branch management obtained a raise that would eliminate her welfare subsidy but which, after deductions, left her total income smaller than before. By joining a union she had everything to gain but she could not afford to lose what little she had in the process. Nevertheless, she did what was right and necessary.

I was so shocked by her treatment that it became a simple matter of wrong and right. The present situation was unequivocally wrong—going against everything I believed was just. So when it came time to join the union, there was no decision to be made. I did what was right and necessary.

We've got to go out and build our union
We've got to build it for ourselves
There ain't nobody going to build it for us
We've got to go out and build our union for ourselves.
— Additional verse to Woody Guthrie's "You've Gotta
go Down and Join the Union"

3   Our Own Local

Within a month of the first application, 104 bank workers joined the union. We were signing bank workers into the union on the basis that it was a democratic union and bank workers would control our own executive, finances and negotiations. We were anxious to form our own local as soon as possible. Those were times of euphoria and exhiliration. We couldn't lose.

On September 26, 1976, the Bank Employees' Organizing Committee asked for and received a charter from the SORWUC National Executive and thereby became the United Bank Workers, Local 2, SORWUC. Our founding meeting was held at the Fishermen's Hall in Vancouver and was attended by thirty bank workers. We elected our first executive: President, Dodie Zerr from Victory Square; Vice-President, Charlotte Johnson from the Commerce Data Center; Secretary, Jackie Ainsworth from Victory Square; Treasurer, Maureen Pearson from the Scotia at SFU; Trustees, Eileen Sprout from the Vancouver Heights Scotia and Barb Dyer, Bank of Montreal, Cloverdale.

In the next few months, we worked on building our local. We set times and places for executive meetings and membership meetings, made provisions for collecting dues, and coordinated our sign-up campaign. We made decisions about what expenses we would be responsible for and what the National Executive should pay, how much our petty cash should be, how much letterhead we should order, what leaflets we needed and who should write them. We established procedures for signing cheques and paying bills. We divided up among ourselves all this work plus: talking to the CLRB investigating officers, signing up our co-workers, talking to the press, meeting with other unions, meeting with our lawyers. And of course, we were all working at the bank. If we weren't at meetings, we were on the phone—talking to bank workers and arranging meetings. It was all really exciting and although relationships at home were suffering, we were building important new ones and we were finally taking on the banks.

UBW Executive members met with other trade unionists to discuss our organizing drive. Some were friendly; others were respectful or hostile or patronizing or wary or excited. To some, the fact that we were not affiliated to the Canadian Labour Congress (CLC) meant a great deal; others didn't seem to care. (The CLC is a national federation of unions—U.S. based trade unions and Canadian public and government employees' unions.) Charlotte Johnson worked the evening shift at the data centre so she often met with trade union leaders during the days and then someone else would speak at union meetings in the evenings.

There were meetings every night of the week, often two in one evening, and there was always the lunch hour when a short meeting could be squeezed in. Not everyone could make it to our meetings and so much was happening that we decided to put out a regular newsletter. It was called "The Monthly Statement."

The CLRB investigating officers arranged to meet us after work when we could go over the various applications, state our position regarding inclusion/exclusion issues, and discuss the procedure for the Board hearings on the bargaining unit question. There were zillions of forms to type for each application for certification.

The investigating officers had been assigned by the Board to inspect the membership forms, to come down to our office to photocopy our membership records for each branch, and photocopy our deposit books proving payment of initiation fees and membership dues. It was important that each person paid the membership fee themselves out of their own money. This, to the Board, proved the person did indeed wish to be represented by the union. The Board assigned one investigating officer for each bank. Once an application went in, the officer assigned to this bank sent us a copy of the reports which the bank had submitted regarding the number of employees in the branch, their positions, the organizational structure and hierarchy, and which positions the bank wanted excluded from the bargaining unit. A bank worker from the branch would come down to the office after work to meet with the officer and verify that the bank's information was correct.

In response to each application, each bank wrote a letter to the Board saying they contested the application on the grounds that one bank branch was not an appropriate bargaining unit. They further stated that in their view, SORWUC should have to prove it was a proper union as defined by the Canadian Labour Code. They argued that loans officers, manager's secretaries, management trainees, and/or part-time employees should be excluded. The banks had the gall to say that part-time employees should not be allowed to join the union because they were not entitled to any bank benefits and therefore had no interest in improving the benefits. We had to answer each of these arguments for each branch we applied for.

There was an awful lot of legal work to be done. The basic rules about organizing banks had not yet been established. SORWUC would be setting legal precedents on questions like: Can banks be organized branch by branch, or must employees of a whole region join the union before it can be recognized? Are loans officers and managers' secretaries employees under the Code and entitled to join the union? How far can management go in persuading employees not to join the union?

SORWUC was for the first time organizing in an industry falling under federal jurisdiction. Unlike most industries, banks, shipping companies, railways, airlines, radio stations and some other transportation and communication enterprises are covered by federal labour legislation. Although SORWUC was already officially recognized by the B.C. Labour Relations Board, we had to prove that we were "a trade union in the meaning of the Act" to the satisfaction of the Canada Labour Relations Board.

At first, we met with Harry Rankin, our lawyer, in the early mornings, on our way to work. When we realized that establishing bank workers' legal right to organize would involve a great deal of legal research and several days of hearings before the CLRB, we were turned over to Ian Donald, a partner in Rankin's firm. We met with Ian after work, on our lunch hours and on weekends.

In the past, although SORWUC had sought advice from lawyers, we had always represented ourselves at the B.C. Labour Relations Board. We didn't feel we could do that with the bank campaign. We were told that the Canada Labour Relations Board was more formal and legalistic than the B.C. Board, and that the banks were likely to appeal Board decisions to the Courts, which made it more important to have everything legally and technically correct. We didn't want to take the chance of losing on some technicality and jeopardizing the jobs of UBW members and the whole organizing campaign. As well, we didn't have time to meet with all the bank workers who wanted to meet with us, and there was no way we wanted to spend our evenings in the law library when we could be organizing more branches. So we began running up a legal bill.

We were communicating by phone and mail with the Canadian Union of Bank Employees (CUBE), another independent union which had applied for four bank branches in southern Ontario around the same time that we applied for Victory Square. They received help in their organizing efforts from the Canadian Chemical Workers Union, a breakaway group from the International Chemical Workers Union. We were thrilled to learn that bank workers in other areas of Canada were also organizing. They faced the same problems we did, and we shared experiences and information as much as we could.

We had signed up seventeen branches by February 3, 1977. Half were in or near Vancouver and the others were mostly on Vancouver Island. At this point it was hard to keep up with the requests for information from bank workers. There were volunteers from Local 1 working in the office on a regular basis, but we decided we needed a full-time office person to work solely for the UBW. Although it would have been best to elect a UBW member to this position, leaves of absence are virtually unheard of in the banks and no one wanted to quit their job at this point. Heather MacNeill, who had been involved in the AUCE organizing drive, agreed to work for us. Her first job had been as a teller at the Royal Bank so she was anxious to be involved in a union drive that was taking on one of her worst employers. UBW members voted in a referendum ballot to hire Heather at $700 per month for six months, and then review the position. AUCE donated $200 per month towards the salary, and we had to raise the other $500. It was a terrible wage but it was more than the starting wage in the banks. In February 1977

Heather became the first person ever to be paid a salary by SORWUC.

Also in February 1977 SORWUC held a national convention. At the beginning, we bank workers were nervous about attending our first union convention. Many UBW members met members of Local 1 for the first time, and heard reports about Electrical Trades Credit Union negotiations, the strike at Mallabar Tuxedo Rentals, the attempt to organize Lifestream Health Food Store, our certification at Bimini Neighbourhood Pub and our application for three outlets of Church's Chicken.

It was exciting to get the whole union together and discover how much we had in common with waitresses who were organizing into Local 1. The fight at Bimini sounded just like what we were up against in the banks. The day after the workers applied for certification, almost everyone withdrew from the union. There was serious division between the women waitresses and the men bartenders. Local 1 had been certified at Bimini and was trying to rebuild union support and prepare for negotiations. We reported to the convention on the formation and growth of the United Bank Workers, Local 2.

The convention passed constitutional amendments and resolutions to solve a technical problem. Bank workers had been joining as members of the National Union when, according to the constitution, we should have been joining Local 2. We expected the banks to use this against us in the hearings.

At this convention, we elected Jean Rands as National President and Elizabeth Godley as National Secretary. Elizabeth took on the responsibility of coordinating the requests for information coming from bank workers outside the Lower Mainland. She coordinated the leaflet drives and meetings in different parts of the province. Elizabeth, Melody and Heather travelled to the Island, the Interior and the Sechelt Peninsula to meet with people. We rented more office space in the Dominion Building and were always bringing in more desks for people to work at. Two more phones were added, and almost monthly we were reorganizing tasks and assignments. The work piled up.

The UBW set up a grievance committee to work on individual complaints. One problem was the banks' practice of deducting money from the tellers' wages when they were short in their cash. At the Scotia, if you were short more than $2 it was necessary that the supervisor count your cash. This was time-consuming and had to be done at the end of the day when people were tired and anxious to get home. So if you were out $2.75, it was not unheard of to slip 75 cents out of your own purse and throw it into your cash in order to avoid a cash count. Quite a set up—the bank had us throwing in our two bits here and there to add to their million dollar profits. Any cash overage was put into a special account at the branch and eventually sent to the Bank of Canada.

If a teller was short more than $2, she had to make up the difference to a maximum of $10. For anything over $10, the teller paid a percentage (generally 10%). The Scotia took $5 a month out of the employee's personal account until the "debt" was paid. This outrageous practice resulted in one teller having her rent cheque bounce. She went on vacation and had left just enough money in her account to cover her rent when the bank put through a $5 debit and her rent cheque was returned NSF. This happened before the union had applied for her branch. The "Monthly Statement" announced that the next time the bank deducted any money from a teller who was a union member, the union would take the case to small claims court. We released our newsletter article to the press. Within two months, each bank announced to all their employees that there would be no further deductions for cash shortages. Although we didn't have a collective agreement and weren't even certified, the fact that we were working together and speaking out as one already meant we had some power.

The grievance committee challenged the banks' use of lie detector tests. We were approached by bank employees who had been subjected to these tests as part of management's investigations of shortages. Although the banks claimed the tests were voluntary, the employees felt their jobs were on the line. We researched and publicized studies which showed the tests were unreliable and intimidating, and American laws which prohibited the use of lie detector tests in employment relationships. We wrote to the Minister of Labour demanding that protective legislation be passed. Again, we released our letter to the press. The Civil Liberties Association of B.C. helped us on this issue.

We were always fighting the myth that it was impossible to organize the banks. In the media blitz following our first application, Opal Skilling, Secretary of Local 15 of the international Office and Technical Employees' Union (OTEU), said SORWUC was bound to fail because in order to apply for an individual branch, it was necessary to change the Bank Act. No wonder bank workers were confused!

Most people thought that the banks were just too big and powerful to be organized (even many who joined the union essentially did so as a protest). Often these feelings were expressed in terms of money of which the banks had unlimited amounts. They would have the best lawyers, negotiators, public relations men, all working against us. Whereas we were just a bunch of women with no strike fund, and very little in the way of dues income. We argued that a bank workers' union would have 120,000 members and would be one of the biggest and most powerful unions in the country. If bank workers wanted a union, lack of money couldn't stop us. Then we set out to prove that that was true.

Most of our organizing work was inexpensive. Our meetings with other bank workers in the Lower Mainland cost nothing. Hundreds of volunteers stood outside bank branches handing out leaflets. We worked hard on press releases and we never bought advertising. Mimeographing, folding, stapling, and mailing were all done by volunteer labour.

Nevertheless, we were soon up to our necks in new expenses: the office space we needed to accommodate volunteers working on the campaign; the two new phones; travelling expenses and long distance calls to sign up distant branches and then keep in touch; tons of paper for newsletters and leaflets; hundreds of dollars in postage each month;

legal expenses and the salary for our one paid union organizer.

We knew it would be a while before we had enough dues coming in from bank workers to cover the salary, rent and phone bills. In fact, our dues covered less than 10% of our expenses. There were two ways of dealing with the continual financial crisis—cutting costs and fund-raising.

We couldn't cut costs where it would defeat our objectives. For instance, we had to pay travelling expenses for out-of-town members to come to meetings because we couldn't build a democratic organization of bank workers any other way. It was difficult for them to use cheap methods of travel because they didn't have enough time. Sometimes, bank workers paid their own way. Sometimes they were able to raise money in their own community.

Volunteers who travelled for the union used the cheapest possible methods—cars, buses, boats, even hitchhiking. (Sometimes we found new organizing possibilities by talking to people we met on buses or while hitchhiking.) But again we faced the same problem as with legal stuff—we didn't want to be spending our time on a bus when we could be signing up more branches.

We rarely spent money on hotels. Staying with other union members or supporters not only saved money but provided opportunities for informal discussion about the union, and the development of new friendships. A UBW organizer on the road would establish a temporary office in some downtown restaurant with a pay phone, stopping there to do paper work and make calls between leafletting, meeting bank workers at noon and after work, doing media interviews and meeting with local union leaders.

We printed tens of thousands of leaflets very cheaply thanks to Press Gang, a women's press in Vancouver. Our letters and newsletters were mailed by volunteer labour.

In spite of all our attempts to save, the two year campaign cost about $85,000. While this was not much money, it seemed a lot to us and fund-raising was a major activity of the union.

We tried to do fund-raising in such a way that it built the campaign generally. Support from other unions would be crucial to bank workers when it came to negotiating and taking job action, as well as in the initial organizing stages. Our main fund-raising method was sending letters to local unions around B.C. In many cases, this was followed up by personal discussions with active members of those unions, or by bank workers speaking at local union meetings.

We were part of the union movement and we needed support and solidarity. It made sense for other unions to help in the organization of this important unorganized industry, but we didn't like to have to be financially dependent on other unions. We hoped it was temporary. With 1000 dues-paying members in the banks we could cover our expenses but for the moment we had to rely on donations from other unions.

The fund-raising activities brought bank workers into contact with experienced unionists who could help in other ways. They gave bank workers more information about unions in general and the union movement in their community. Over two years we raised about $30,000 in donations and interest-free loans from other unions Over 100 local unions in B.C. contributed. The unions that were the most generous were relatively small independent unions, because they understood our

---

The following unions donated to our organizing campaign in B.C. We apologize for any errors or omissions.

Amalgamated Transit Union (ATU)

Association of University and College Employees (AUCE): Local 1, Local 2, Local 3, Local 4 and Provincial

Bakery Confectionary and Tobacco Workers International Union, Local 475

B.C. Ferry & Marine Workers Union

B.C. Government Employees Union (BCGEU): Provincial and Administrative Support Component

B.C. Projectionists Union

Canadian Airline Flight Attendants Association

Canadian Association of Industrial Mechanical and Allied Workers (CAIMAW) Local 6

Canadian Association of Smelter and Allied Workers (CASAW)

Canadian Brotherhood of Railway, Transport and General Workers (CBRT &GW), Local 400 Seamen's Section

CBRT&GW Local 276

Canadian Paperworkers Union (CPU), Local 76, Local 456, Local 592, Local 603, Local 686, Local 789, Local 1092, Local 1119, Local 1132

Canadian Union of Postal Workers (CUPW), locals in Vancouver, Kelowna, Mackenzie, New Westminster, Port Alberni, Powell River, Prince Rupert, Terrace, Trail

Canadian Union of Public Employees (CUPE). Local 881, Local 379, Local 439, Local 606, Local 626, Local 695, Local 718, Local 723, Local 728, Local 900, Local 1760

Carpenters and Joiners, Local 1598, Local 1696, Local 1998, Local 2511, Local 3014

Cement Lime & Gypsum Workers

Distillery Workers, Local 604, Retail Wholesale & Department Store Union

Hospital Employees Union (HEU)

International Brotherhood of Electrical Workers (IBEW), Local 213, Local 1003, Local 2354

International Woodworkers of America (IWA), Local 1-217, Local 1-367, Local 1-363, Local 1-80, Local 1-118, Local 1-405, Local 1-417

Ladies Auxiliary Kamloops, Regional Council No. 1

Labourers International Union Local 1093

Letter Carriers Union of Canada (LCUC), Local 12, Local 32, Local 170, Local 172, Local 270

Machinists

National Association of Broadcast Employees & Technicians (NABET) Local 84

Newspaper Guild

Oil Chemical and Atomic Workers Local 9-675

Plumbers Pipefitters and Steamfitters, Local 170

Public Service Alliance of Canada (PSAC) Local 20169, Local 20043

Pulp Paper and Woodworkers of Canada (PPWC), Local 2, Local 3, Local 4, Local 8, Local 9, Local 10, Local 11, Local 15, Local 18 and National

Social Service Employees Union Local 2 (VMREU)

United Fishermen and Allied Workers Union (UFAWU), Local 1, Local 2, Local 4, Local 8, Local 10, Local 21, Local 26, Local 31, Local 42, Local 99

United Transportation Union (UTU), Local 1051

Vancouver Municipal and Regional Employees Union (VMREU)

needs more, although they could afford it less. AUCE, an organization consisting mostly of women clerical workers at universities and colleges in B.C., saw that in the long run they could be successful at improving conditions for their members only if clerical workers in the private sector were organized. Over the next two years they gave us over $15,000 in donations and interest-free loans for the bank campaign, as well as donations to SORWUC Local 1 strike fund. The Pulp Paper and Woodworkers of Canada (PPWC) gave us over $8,000 in donations and interest-free loans. PPWC is affiliated to the Confederation of Canadian Unions (CCU), an alternative organization to the Canadian Labour Congress (CLC), formed by independent unions in opposition to the "international" (American) unions which dominate the CLC. We received $5,250 from the Vancouver Municipal and Regional Employees Union (VMREU), another small, independent union.

We spoke at meetings of women's groups and NDP meetings. The amount of money from each meeting was small, but it did add up. At those meetings we met people who agreed to help in other ways—by handing out leaflets, helping with mailings and other office work, putting us in touch with bank workers they knew and with other organizations. We raised about $3,000 from organizations other than unions, and $3,000 from individuals.

We asked individual supporters, union locals and other organizations to pledge a certain amount on a monthly basis, so we would be in a position to budget to some extent rather than going from crisis to crisis. We weren't terribly successful, partly because we were so busy organizing we never found the time to establish our fund-raising on an efficient basis.

For the first seven months, our income generally increased along with our membership. By March, we had signed up twenty-two branches, and donations were coming in at the rate of almost $900 per month.

Now if you want equal wages let me tell you what you do
You got to work with your sisters in the shop with you.
If we all stick together now it won't be long. . .
We'll open up new jobs. . .win equal pay. . .make that seniority list.
— Barbara Wertheimer, "Talking Union"

4 Talking Union

As a result of publicity about the union application at Victory Square, we met bank employees who had tried for years to organize. One of these employees was Charlotte Johnson. Here she tells about organizing in the data centres:

In February 1969, I started at the Commerce Data Centre as a machine operator. The machine looked like an old adding machine. By punching the keys, I encoded amounts and account numbers onto debits and credits of the numerous Commerce branches. I also added code numbers for service chargeable or non-service chargeable items. The items were designated as recurring debits or credits, blocked accounts, demand loan interest payments, or safety deposit box charges. When a new branch goes on computer, the balance of every account at that bank has to be fed into the computer; after that only the daily transactions need be entered.

There were easily 100 of us in one room, with about seventy-five noisy machines. It was impossible to talk, and the machines made it unbearably hot. In August, I became a reconciler. Reconciliation involves working with the computer print-out, correcting errors and balancing the branch totals. Although I was no longer working on a machine, I still worked in the same big room.

Staff morale was very low and the turnover very high. Supervisors treated the employees like they were liabilities to the company. When employees in my department voiced complaints, they were told: "All fifty of you can quit if you don't like it here and we'll hire fifty more tomorrow." (Too bad everyone didn't take them up on it!)

I resigned in the summer of 1970 and was hired at the Royal Data Centre. There were so many former Commerce employees working at the Royal, it was like old home week. The encoding machines used at the Royal had sixteen pockets (bins). The machine operators encoded the amount of the debit or credit and then pressed a number indicating the category of the item (other bank's cheques, family allowance cheques, travelers cheques, deposits, etc.). These cheques and deposits would be automatically sorted to the proper pocket. When the bin was full it would pop open. The operator would then take a total on that bin, record the total and remove the items. At the end of the shift, the operator would punch in all the totals (+debits, -credits) and balance. All bins then had to be totaled out for the next shift. The job was production. You had to be fast and accurate. If we didn't balance, we were supposed to punch out on time cards until we found the error, then punch in again. Management wanted to know exactly how much of our shift we spent on production. We were treated like children and, like at the Commerce, the turnover was high.

I quit the Royal when I was going to have a new member in the family. As I was not "working" all I had to do was cook, clean house, wash clothes, sew and mend, chauffeur, shop, nurse, change diapers, iron and fold clothes, cut the lawn, garden, counsel, listen to and generally take care of a family of five. While I was enjoying the extra leisure time at home, a co-worker from the Commerce who was now a supervisor phoned several times asking me to return to the Commerce. She said I would notice a big change. I agreed to return but only as a part-time reconciler working two or three nights a week. Because the shift started at 5:45 p.m., it was possible to feed the kids supper before going to work. It was now February, 1974. Big changes! The only change was the new supervisors. Bank policy was bank policy and the bosses in Toronto were unreachable. We started talking union.

There were many grievances which led up to the union talk. Our shift supposedly ended at 12:45 a.m. If the volume of work was excessive, the employees would work overtime to get the items back to the branch for the next business day. If it was impossible to complete all the work, the items could be held over and backdated one day. When there was a holdover, the employees would have the previous day's holdover to complete in addition to the new day's transactions. If the systems were down or if deliveries were delayed, that also meant late nights. Nobody was asked if they wanted to work overtime. We were expected to work overtime and couldn't go home until we were dismissed. However, if the employees finished early they could leave and still be paid for the full shift. Sound like a good deal? The employees really pushed to get out early and on heavy nights, pushed even harder so they could get out of there before 2 or 3 a.m. So no matter what the volume of work was, the employees were always working at full speed.

Maximum production and computer time were the only interests management had. Half of the people in my department were part-time employees like myself. Some had been there as long as ten years. We got none of the regular benefits—no seniority, no sick leave, no medical plan, no pension plan. Some people had their hours cut arbitrarily and without warning while others were forced to resign because their hours were increased. Days off were changed without consultation or notice.

At one time management decided part-time employees would only be paid for hours worked, while the full-time employees would still be paid for the full shift if they finished early. At the coffee break, the full-time people were rushing to get back to work so that they could push the work through and get home early. The part-time people said that there was no way they were going to push themselves because then they wouldn't get paid for the full shift. Everyone started out in a kidding mood but it soon became heated. We could see that this new policy was creating a division between full-time and part-time people so we decided to do something before it went any further. The part-time employees were scheduled to work heavy nights. If they happened to get an early night once in a while it was felt that they deserved it. With the support of all the employees, we went on a slow down. This caused problems with computer time and management restored the benefit to the part-time workers immediately.

Another grievance was secret pay cheques. You worked your butt off on increasing your production to get a $1.00 per night raise. Then you found out that the new employee with no experience that you'd been training started at $2.00 more per shift than you made. The supervisors used to hand out the pay slips but when we started discussing our wages, the pay slips were put in envelopes marked "private and confidential" and we were told not to discuss them.

Promotions went to employees who socialized with the supervisors, without regard for seniority or ability. Job vacancies were kept secret. Employees needing medical leaves were asked to resign. They would be rehired but with loss of benefits and loss of seniority for holidays, etcetera. A seven year employee was in a car accident and should have been able to recover without a worry because she had accrued sick time. Management asked for her resignation. I had heard that "the bank never fires anyone". Well they sure asked for a lot of resignations.

When the union talk started most of the employees thought that bank employees could not belong to a union. When I was trying to locate the proper union to join, I was told by the international OTEU that we could not join a union. I was mad! What right did they have to say bank workers couldn't join a union? I then talked to the Canadian Union of Public Employees (CUPE) and was told we could join a union but the Labour Board would probably reject it if it was with an international union. CUPE put the Association of Commercial and Technical Employees (ACTE) in touch with me and we were off (or so we thought).

The ACTE organizing drive began in February 1975 and it went surprisingly well at first. The Data Centre employed about 375 people of whom sixty-seven were manager, assistant manager, department heads, supervisors or assistant supervisors. It was a hard place to organize as different shifts had almost no contact with one another. Employees were divided not only by shifts but by departments, rooms, and floors. We knew that to be successful we had to get people on the different shifts organized.

Myself and another part-time worker, Janette Hegglin, signed up our fellow workers. We would visit people at home or take them out for coffee. When we had signed a majority in one department, we moved on to the next one. In the first month, Janette and I signed up fifty-four people. I still have that wonderful list.

We held our first meeting March 16, 1975 at a hotel in Burnaby.

Then all hell broke loose!

The assistant manager, the new personnel manager, and the shift manager came to my department and stood with their arms folded across their chests watching the employees do their work. This went on every night for two weeks and the employees were very jumpy and afraid to be seen talking with Janette or myself.

An administrative officer came right out and asked one employee if she had started the union drive. This employee had previously been demoted when a friend of a supervisor was given her job. She had then had a nervous breakdown and was off work for three months. I guess they thought she had good reason to unionize.

Management and supervisors of all shifts had a meeting and came out with a list of possible union organizers—all the employees they knew to be unhappy with working conditions. (I bet it was a long one.) A friendly supervisor phoned to tell me that Janette and I were on the list and that we were considered the main organizers.

Employees were called into the office individually and questioned as to how much they knew about the union and whether or not they were members.

Clara had not received her pay cheque for six weeks due to a foulup in Payroll. They could have made up a cheque manually but instead kept promising "the next pay day". Clara phoned me and said that usually she sat on the fence but since she felt she was getting shafted by the bank she wanted to join the union. It was at her request that I signed her up. She was called into the office by our supervisor. He said, "I understand that you were pressured into joining the union." He was fishing and she jumped for the bait. She agreed she was indeed pressured and when the supervisor asked who did the pressuring, she said, "Charlotte".

Ruth, a part-time employee, was told by a friend who was a branch manager with the Royal, that if she became involved with the union she would be blacklisted. She phoned to warn me that maybe I should also withdraw from the union.

Ruth was called in to the personnel manager's office regarding a staff loan even though we had been told that part-time employees not eligible for staff loans. She was given a loan but she also gave the manager a list of employees who had attended the meeting at the hotel and named the executive. This meeting had been for whoever was interested and not just members. When I asked Ruth about this later, she dismissed it by saying it didn't matter because management knew who they were anyway. Even though I knew that my co-workers were frightened I was annoyed with them. Some of them were falling all over themselves to spill all.

Rhonda, a supervisor, and Marilyn, her assistant and good friend, were told by management that they were not considered management and were encouraged to speak against the union and to try to get people to withdraw from the union. Rhonda agreed to do this and even told some of us, "I care nothing for the friggin' girls, only my career." She told everyone the union organizers would be fired. The employees were also told that the data centre would close down and work would be flown to Toronto. That would have been something to see! First the computers would have to be programmed to take B.C. branches. Secondly, since we had a hard time getting our own branches done on time and wouldn't know what to do with all of the East's, it would have been interesting indeed to see what Toronto would do with ours.

Management cut Janette's and my days down, so we both applied for full-time jobs. They hoped and even suggested that we quit. Since they didn't want to hire us full-time, and were hesitant about hiring new employees ahead of us, our department became very short-staffed. Some co-workers asked us to withdraw our full-time applications so the bank would hire more employees. But we said no, that both of us were experienced and capable employees and we wanted full-time work. Finally management hired two new employees in another department, then transferred them into our department.

I was not at work the night the two employees started but I was scheduled to work the next. When Janette went into the office to find out why inexperienced people had been hired when she had seven years experience and had been requesting full-time work for several months—she was fired—for questioning the decision of her supervisors! I was called at home by my supervisor at 10 p.m. and told not to come to work until the following week. I figured they didn't want me around stirring up trouble about Janette's firing. Janette filed an Unfair Labour Practice complaint through ACTE.

All along, the ACTE reps' attitude was that they would give the organizing a try but it was very unlikely we could do it. This made organizing difficult. They had said to me: "We don't want you to get off the merry-go-round if we take this on." Janette and I put our jobs on the line and Janette lost hers. The ACTE reps never committed themselves or any of the CLC's "million dollar white collar organizing fund" we would hear so much about later. Only once did they hand out leaflets—ACTE booklets which meant nothing to the bank workers. I wrote a leaflet dealing with some bank workers' problems because ACTE said they would have it printed and handed out, but after I gave it to them I never saw it again. We knew the organizing was finished when we gave the reps a list of 110 data centre employees to help sign up and they visited maybe two of them in three months. Just before Janette was fired we had been talking about approaching another union but we didn't know which one.

I saw an article in the newspaper about a lunch hour meeting at the Vancouver Public Library put on by SORWUC, a union interested in organizing women. This certainly caught my attention. I attended the meeting and Janette and I decided to approach SORWUC after her complaint was settled.

The complaint was not settled until July, 1976 (Janette had been fired in January) when she got an out of court settlement. Part of the settlement was that I be given full-time employment. The ACTE rep said, "Keep in touch". That was it.

Shortly after this, we read in the paper that SORWUC had applied for certification at the Commerce Victory Square branch. It was very exciting! We were right about SORWUC being interested in bank workers. I contacted them, went to a meeting and soon was up to my eyebrows in organizing again.

Working with people in SORWUC was a whole different experience. I didn't have to try and convince them that a union was needed in the banks. They were working there, and were experiencing the same difficulties, unfairness, poor working conditions and wages that I was. And it didn't matter which chartered bank, our stories were similar. Working with SORWUC and the other unions that were giving them their support, I understood what trade unionism and solidarity meant.

However, there had been a lot of changes at the Data Centre since the ACTE organizing drive. The on-line computer system in the branches was doing away with many jobs and the employees were afraid to join the union because the job situation was so unstable. Management brought in workers from temporary agencies instead of hiring new employees. Management assured people that there would be no layoffs but we didn't have much faith in what they were saying and when employees were transferred to jobs they didn't like, they didn't complain but were thankful to still be working. Management was not taking employees' wishes into consideration. They brought in a career counselor but nothing ever came of it. We were told we could have three minutes with him, that's how much our "careers" mattered.

We wrote a leaflet for Data Centre employees and SORWUC members leafletted the Centre several times. We held meetings, phoned employees at home and knocked on doors. Those who had actively supported ACTE usually joined SORWUC (although some of them asked for their $5.00 ACTE membership fee back). Those who had passively watched the ACTE drive fizzle out were not about to support yet another organizing drive. Meetings were attended by fewer and fewer people. When we applied for the Scotia Data Centre, the Commerce Data Centre employees said "let's wait and see what happens there and see what they get before we join."

Shortly after the UBW leafletted the Scotia Data Centre some employees contacted the union office. We were very pleased with the response and a meeting was set up at the home of one of the employees. At the first meeting the employees discussed reasons for wanting to join a union—better wages, a dental plan, grievance procedure, protection for part-time workers, regular coffee breaks, and shift differential.

At the Scotia, the employees on afternoon shift were all part-time with the exception of one full-time employee. Her job was to trouble check—if one of the machine operators didn't balance or was having problems she assisted them. Machine operators were paid by piece work—so many items for so many dollars. New employees were expected to average 900 to 1000 items per hour after three months and experienced employees about 1300 per hour. To receive an increment, employees would have to increase their production average and hold that average for three months. If your production dropped for three months your wages would drop accordingly. All employees received the annual cost-of-living increases.

The majority of employees worked afternoon shift, 6:00 p.m. to 1:00 a.m. They had the same system of working until the work was finished as the Commerce, except the Scotia employees received no regular coffee break.

By the time we had a few more meetings several more employees had been signed up. There was no way of getting an exact number of employees working at the Centre but the organizers estimated eighty-five. I stressed that we should sign up a majority of employees before we applied for certification. Otherwise the Board would order a vote and the several months of waiting would give management several months for anti-union activity and I already knew what they could do.

When we finally applied for union certification on February 28, 1977, we did not have a majority. Nevertheless we were really pleased about our first application for a data centre. Our press conference was given by myself and two Scotia data centre employees. Press people were packed into our union office. We told them that the work done at the data centres was crucial and "a 24-hour shut down of the data centres would cripple the B.C. banking industry." We explained that we had joined the UBW because it is an independent union committed to maintaining democracy in the union and we called on all bank workers to join with us in our struggle for better wages and working conditions.

If anyone should ask of you your union to sell
Just tell them where to go, send them back to hell
Get thee behind me Satan, travel on down the line
I am a union woman, going to leave that devil behind.
— The Almanac Singers "Get Thee Behind me Satan"
(slightly rewritten)

5 The Anti-Union Campaign

As our sign-up campaign across the province got into full swing, those opposed to the union also geared up. One group—bank management—we assumed would oppose the union. We were even prepared for them to put up a ferocious anti-union campaign. What we were not prepared for was that some employees would buckle under so quickly and that a few would turn on the union. Initially, these people argued on an individual level with pro-union people but did not actively oppose the pro-union choice of their co-wokrers. They joined the anti-union campaign only when they were convinced there were rewards involved in doing so, or punishment in not doing so.

As the union drive progressed the arguments for and against the union became more complex. Originally, the anti-union employees told us that joining the union was illegal (against the Bank Act), that the banks were just too powerful to allow a union and that we were crazy. They said unions were run by corrupt men who drove Cadillacs and went around ordering people out on strike. We got ourselves copies of the Bank Act and found it had nothing in it about unions. We distributed leaflets and argued about what kind of union SORWUC is.

Dorothy Hooper and Bonnie Wong, the employees sent to Victory Square from Regional Office, set about organizing the opposition. The anti-union employees at Victory Square had buttons and leaflets printed in the name of Bankers Independent Group (BIG). The core of the group was the most senior employees and the supervisors at Victory Square and, of course, Hooper and Wong. Victory Square remained the centre of anti-union activity. Later, BIG got in touch with some employees at the Scotia Data Centre who wrote some leaflet articles. But BIG never really consisted of more than the Victory Square people.

At one point during the campaign we came into work and found BIG leaflets on our desks. As the leaflets were there before the regular mail arrived, we suspected they had been sent via inter-branch mail. The union filed a complaint charging management complicity in the distribution of these anti-union leaflets. We later withdrew the charge for lack of evidence; no one seemed to know how the leaflets had arrived at the branches. (Occasionally the union office received calls about these leaflets. "I just got this terrible leaflet opposed to a union in the banks. I didn't know there was a union in the banks. How do I join?")

There were regular staff meetings (compulsory attendance on company time) where the branch manager would give a "progress report" on the union drive and outline what would happen if we went union. They told us that unions meant everyone had to follow a book of rules, that things would be regimented, that we might have to punch a time clock, and lose our flexible hours (i.e. unpaid overtime!), and we would no longer be able to speak for ourselves (i.e. one teller against the whole bank!)—the union would do it for us. Commerce employees were given a memo eight pages long with questions and answers concerning unions.

The union's main method for communicating with bank workers and answering management memos and anti-union rumours was through the media. We wrote the statements ourselves. We were honest and we were bank workers doing the telling. The press liked us. We were called the "feisty little union", "David", and so forth. We spoke on hotline shows, did feature interviews on TV and in the papers. Whether it was CBC National News or the local community station, we were anxious to talk, to argue about a union in the banks. BIG did only one press release that we know of. The banks are always close-mouthed with the press. So basically we had the media to ourselves.

Our leaflets were also an important means of reaching bank workers. It took lots of energy to write the leaflets, type and lay them out, find graphics, and get them to the printers. Press Gang printed beautiful leaflets for us at cost, otherwise our printing bill would have been astronomical.

Over the years, SORWUC had built quite a leafletting network. It was at its peak during the bank drive. There were tens of thousands of leaflets distributed throughout the province, by women's groups, trade unionists, teachers, NDPers, and many non-aligned supporters. Local 1 members did most of the leafletting in Vancouver and spent long hours organizing leaflet distribution. Each leaflet had a small coupon on the bottom to return to the union office and eventually we stapled membership forms to each leaflet.

But our access to unorganized bank workers couldn't compare with that of bank management. In branches where we had applied for certification, we argued with the manager but in those branches where we had no members, it was his show completely. Even where we did speak up we were at a disadvantage in terms of status. Who would believe us—we were only the employees whereas they were "the bosses"; they had "the money".

When the union office got word that the manager was calling a meeting about the union we would often call the manager and threaten him with an unfair labour practice complaint. We would read to him those sections of the Canada Labour Code that prohibit employers from intimidating employees or interfering in the formation of a trade union. We got the usual answer each time we wrote or called: "I'm a human being. I have a right to express my opinion. Don't you people believe in freedom of speech? This is a free country". We were warned against filing an unfair labour practice complaint about these meetings on the grounds that the bank would appeal to the federal court to get a definitive and bad precedent on employers' rights to "freedom of speech".

The banks used a standard tactic of employers faced with a union campaign—some sudden improvements in conditions and benefits. A dental plan was announced; we got new electric typewriters to replace the manuals; we got new calculators, more adding machines, extra staff, and a new policy of no more deductions for teller cash shortages. In the Commerce they threw in two coffee breaks a day and at the Bank of Montreal they instituted a job posting procedure. They told us that, unfortunately, because of the Anti-Inflation Board they couldn't give us a big raise, but as soon as the wage guidelines were lifted the possibilities were endless.

The union tried to counter the banks' propaganda by mailing to union representatives a regular report of our own to be circulated in the branch. "The Weekly Bulletin" was mailed each Monday. It was a one or two page update of the previous week's activities: legal battles we had won or lost, interesting phone calls, a running tally on branches we had applied for, notices of meetings and later, progress reports on negotiations. Sometimes we included copies of significant letters we had received from other unions or the banks. This, while it was the best that could be done from the union office, had hardly any effect. The fiercest battle was fought in the branch among the employees.

It was not difficult to figure out who was pro or anti union, especially when we were individually confronted by loans officers or supervisors and asked to sign letters or petitions against the union. Although loans officers and supervisors were employees and we wanted to have them included in the bargaining unit, they were seen as representatives of management. The personal supervisory authority that employees have over each other is bolstered by the wage differential between employees. The ratio was as high as three to one among employees within the bargaining unit. It was not uncommon to find a branch manager (a position excluded from the bargaining unit) get promoted to a larger branch as a loans officer (a position included in the bargaining unit). No wonder loans officers often felt more in common with branch managers—their wages and lifestyles were more like managers' than tellers'.

In the couple of months immediately preceding the CLRB hearings, the union office regularly received letters of resignation from members.

Oct. 24, 1976

Dodie Zerr, President,
Sorwuc Local 2
#1114 - 207 W. Hastings
Vancouver, B.C.

Dear Dodie :

Having given this considerable thought,
I have come to the conclusion I must
withdraw my membership from S.O.R.W.U.C.

My decision is governed by several factors,
but the main ones are purely personal. I
feel very strongly that my job of 17 years
standing is in jeopardy and, having to
support my husband, this has swayed
my judgement. Also the great worry of a
terminally ill parent. I find I'm just
not able to cope with this controversial
issue.

Nonetheless, I wish you every success
in your endeavours, but personally feel
the time is not quite "ripe" for us
Bankers in B.C.!

Nov. 7/76

Dear Dodie

Please accept this as my resignation
from S.O.R.W.U.C.

As this is a fairly small community, the
opportunities for employment are fairly
limited, and should the Commerce close
its branch on this island (as has been
rumoured) I am not prepared to start
looking for new employment at this time.
I sincerely wish you every success in
trying to get the banks unionized.

We were afraid to open the mail. The letters reflected, in different ways, management's interference in our choice to join the union. Several of the letters from different branches in different parts of B.C. were identically worded, including the same spelling error in the first sentence. During one set of CLRB hearings, when questioned by the union lawyer, an employee who had signed one of the protest letters admitted that she had got the letter from her supervisor who had got it from an employee at Victory Square.

People were promised long awaited transfers and promotions. They were told that these promotions or transfers couldn't, of course, take effect until this union mess was cleaned up. They said that the sooner people withdrew from the union, the sooner it would be cleaned up.

The banks also zeroed in on individual employees. At the Ganges branch of the Commerce they decided it was necessary, because of the shortage of work, to "lay-off" Chris, the head teller and union activist. They told her she could re-apply in a few months if there was a vacancy. At the same time they announced that a management trainee was coming from Vancouver to train at the branch. We filed a complaint with the CLRB. The bank decided it had all been a mistake and they had never meant to "lay-off" Chris. At Port McNeill the bank decided that Susan, one of their part-time employees, and a union member, was no longer needed at the branch. The union members in the branch reacted angrily and quickly. There were frantic phone calls back and forth between the members in the branch, the union office, the lawyers, and the Regional Office. It had all been a mistake. The bank had never meant to "lay-off" Susan.

At Victory Square, Dodie and Jackie were moved from the ledgers department to the teller line. Our lawyer said it was not an unfair labour practice because there was no "pecuniary loss"—the bank continued to pay them at the same rate. However, people in the branch saw going from a desk job to being on cash as a serious demotion, even if the pay was the same. One of the tellers who had withdrawn from the union was given Jackie's ledger position.

Sometimes the opposite occurred and it worked just as well in unsettling the branch. That is, sometimes the union activists were promoted out of the bargaining unit. In one branch, one of the main union activists went from ledgerkeeper to accountant, a management position.

In some branches where employees had regularly been leaving at 4:30, the supervisors required that we stay and do filing until 5 p.m. saying that this would "give us a taste of what it would be like when the union got in". In some branches there was a freeze on hiring. When an employee quit she was not replaced. In a couple of branches this reached a ridiculous point and people became frantic with overwork. Management said that until this union mess was cleaned up, Regional Office would not send anyone new to the branch.

Tension in the branches was high and personal harassment common. Rather than withdraw from the union, some people quit in disgust.

But this had the same practical effect as withdrawing—there was one less union member in an already small unit.

We were shocked at the reaction of some of the more senior staff. One paragraph of a leaflet we distributed called "Let's Work Together" describes our feelings: "Senior staff have the most to gain from unionization—proper job postings, orderly and fair promotion procedures, longer vacations, monetary recognition of skill and seniority, and a union grievance procedure. . . . The union understands that some managers are upset at the possible loss of arbitrary personal authority from unionization; but we are amazed that some senior clerical staff, whose incomes are considerably less than those of unskilled workers in union jobs, should campaign against the union. Instead, as bank employees we should be working together to democratically determine our proposals for wages and working conditions."

We preferred to meet anti-union employees head on. When there was division in the branches, we encouraged union and anti-union people to get together and debate the issue. On an issue by issue basis, we generally won. In branches where this debate did occur, the tension was eased whether or not individuals changed their minds about the union.

BIG didn't like debates. In one branch the loans officer had set up a branch meeting on a Saturday morning to which he invited some BIG people. Union members in the branch contacted the union office and invited union people to come also. When we showed up at the meeting, BIG refused to debate with us. Because BIG wouldn't debate, this meeting allowed one-half hour for BIG people to speak and then half an hour for union representatives. It didn't look good for BIG. If the union people were willing to stay and debate, what was BIG afraid of?

Bonnie Wong also made a trip to Kamloops where she met with branch employees, sometimes on company time, usually at the bank, to talk to them about the union. In one of these Kamloops meetings, she described how a SORWUC cheque had bounced on a union member's personal account at the Victory Square branch. Presumably she was trying to demonstrate the union's sad financial state, something we had never kept secret. However, this cheque had been bounced in error and the manager of our credit union later apologized. Wong's mistake was in publicly discussing the confidential details of a customer account—a serious offense for any bank employee. We sued her for libel. This action effectively ended Wong's anti-union activities. The suit was later dropped but it had the desired effect.

The union members in Port McNeill wrote a leaflet for distribution to Kamloops branches. Wong had told bank workers in Kamloops that "happy" branches had become divided and torn once they had applied for union certification. The Port McNeill leaflet said: "Not everyone in our branch has decided to join the union, but this has not disrupted the manner in which the branch runs—in fact, staff turnover has decreased since we decided to unionize, making for a smoother running branch. We did not join SORWUC out of spite towards our manager or because we disliked our jobs—we like our work but we want to improve our working situation."

In branches where the supervisors were pro-union we hardly ever heard of any problems until after they had been solved. In a Bank of Montreal branch, where the main union activists were the most senior employees, the manager tried to break up their group by re-scheduling their coffee breaks. For over ten years this group had been taking their coffee together each morning. When the manager tried to split them up, he was told that what he was doing was against the Labour Code. The chief clerk removed the coffee break schedule the manager had posted and placed it on her desk in full view along with a copy of the Labour Code. The manager was invited to discuss it with her whenever he liked. He never did get around to talking to her about it and coffee breaks went on as they always had.

Heavy intimidation in the branches often wore down union members as the days and weeks and months went by. In some cases the gap between the application and the hearings was eight months. There was then a further wait before certification. When calling the union office, the first thing bank workers said after hello was: is there a date set for the hearing yet?

At a general membership meeting on March 17, 1977, we decided that if the CLRB didn't contact us within two weeks with a date for our hearing, we would hold a press conference to protest the delay. We had been respectfully silent about the Canada Labour Relations Board up to that time. They had an important hearing to arrange and we didn't want to rush them. Besides, they had a lot of power and we didn't want to antagonize them. But our first branch had applied for certification seven months before and there was still no word of a hearing date. The number of new members had decreased considerably since the new year—everyone was waiting for the decision.

A week after the general meeting we got the word. The hearings were to be held in Vancouver the week of April 18, 1977.

People together have power
Now is the hour to use our strength wisely
Sharing and caring and winning the right to beginning
To live out a life for ourselves.
  — "Song For Ourselves" based on Chris Williamson's
  "Song of the Soul"

6   The Hearings

The hearings began April 18, 1977 on the seventh floor of a federal government office building at 750 Cambie Street in Vancouver. The hearing room had tables set up in one large square. At the front of the room were three large chairs for the Board members. On one side was a chair for the secretary; on the other a chair for the witness. Along the back table, facing the Board, were chairs for all the lawyers. The tables were equipped with microphones, shiny pitchers and water glasses.

Behind the square were rows of chairs for spectators, and at the back of the room, a recording table. The spectators' chairs were filled. We had arranged time off for a rep from each branch and the officers of the UBW to attend the hearings. The union paid our wages. There were always about a dozen bank workers present.

Outside the hearing room was a room with vinyl couches, ceramic coffee tables and a speaker system so that the proceedings could be heard. Three or four adjoining offices were used for caucus meetings.

Dodie Zerr describes the hearings.

We had never laid eyes on any of the bank's big shots, their lawyers or the Board members before. That first day, there they all were, congregated in the outer room.

The bankers and their lawyers talked as if the Board was impertinent to have bothered them at all—and to hold the hearings in Vancouver just didn't make sense. After all, Commerce Court is in Toronto, and they are busy men. Nevertheless, there they were in their grey suits, with gold watches and fat briefcases. At long last we were meeting the gents who were not only our bosses, but were close to the boys who ran the fiscal fibres of our country. All I could think of was how much money they made, and the trouble we were causing them.

The bank's lawyers were two senior partners from a fancy law firm in Toronto. They had a Vancouver lawyer to assist them. All the banks —Commerce, Montreal, Scotia, and Toronto-Dominion—had the same lawyers, and presumably the same position on the bargaining unit question. The Board was going to start by hearing the eight branches of the Commerce. While each bank would thereafter be heard separately, subsequent decisions would be determined by that first historic decision.

For the last few weeks we had been frantically preparing for this moment. Ian Donald, our lawyer, and articling student Peter Doherty were working full-time on the case. We spent many hours with them going over testimony and preparing for cross-examination of the bank's witnesses. We were nervous, but proud and confident that our twenty applications showed this was no flash in the pan but the beginning of a big campaign. We felt that this time the Board would have to lay out the rules for organizing the banks.

In the branches, we had our first taste of legitimacy. Union members attended the hearings as the representatives of employees in their branch. The fight was not between SORWUC and BIG, as management had tried to make out. The fight was between the union and the banks.

After a meeting between the Board members and the lawyers, the hearings got under way. Three members of the CLRB sat facing the bank's lawyers, our lawyers and Bonnie Wong's lawyer. Because we had raised the issue of anti-union activities at Victory Square, Wong attended each day of the hearings with observer status.

The hearing room was packed with SORWUC members and supporters, other trade unionists, management types from other banks and from credit unions and trust companies, and reporters. The Board, in consultation with the lawyers, decided to hear evidence and argument on whether a branch was an appropriate bargaining unit first. Then they would proceed to the issues of whether SORWUC was a proper trade union, whether we had a majority in each branch, whether there had been improper conduct on the part of bank management, and which positions in each branch should be included in the bargaining unit.

The Chairman of the Board began by outlining the reports of the investigating officers on each of the branches—how many employees in each branch, which positions were being contested by the union or the bank, whether or not the union had a majority. He also outlined the structure of the Commerce as a whole—fourteen regions in the country, 1693 branches in Canada (114 outside Canada), 243 branches in B.C., 3900 full-time and part-time employees in B.C. including 1800 in Greater Vancouver.

The lawyers made their opening remarks. Ian's speech was extensively quoted in the press. He said it was amazing that the banks had avoided collective bargaining to date. Was that because of the bank's great generosity in providing fantastic salaries and great benefits? That was doubtful. Part of the fault might lie with the labour movement. But mostly it was because of the bank's successful efforts in killing any attempts at organizing.

"The basic reason why there has been no collective representation at the bank, I suggest, is a myth that banks are immune from trade union representation. . . . Together with that myth there is a fear of loss of jobs, loss of job advancement and its concomitant feeling of helplessness in the face of large and powerful institutions . . . ."

"There must, in our respectful view, be a clear message transmitted throughout Canada that a bank can indeed be certified, for only then will the fears be allayed and the immunity myth destroyed."

The bank's lawyer was brief. He said that the bank was responsible and responsive to its employees and customers and described the banking industry as a highly sensitive critical mechanism. He said that his evidence would show the complexity of the banking structure. He also warned that he would argue that the Board should **not** decide on another unit if the union was unsuccessful in its bid for branch by branch certification. This would have forced us to guess again. Knowing only that the branch was not a unit, we would have to organize, say, the whole province and apply for certification without knowing whether the province was a unit or not.

The presentation of SORWUC's evidence began after lunch. Jean Rands, National President, was our first witness. She described the formation and goals of SORWUC, the history of the bank drive, and why we thought the branch was an appropriate unit. Through Jean's answers to Ian's questions, we put forward our case that bank workers did not in practice have the right to organize because the bargaining unit had never been determined. Jean talked about how how hard it was to sign up bank workers when we had to admit that we didn't even know the rules of the game yet.

She defended our actions in applying for certification for branch units even though we were having second thoughts about that bargaining unit. The day before the hearing started, a UBW special membership meeting voted that "in terms of the objectives of our union, the province would be the best bargaining unit." This motion was the result of intense anti-union pressure in the branches, the difficulty of maintaining majorities in individual branches, and our feeling that bank workers organized on a province wide basis would have more bargaining power. Already we felt we could take on a larger unit.

Jean mostly argued that the Board had to define a bargaining unit so that bank workers would know they had the right to organize. She had quite a debate with the bank's lawyer on this. He argued that the union had told bank employees through thousands of bulletins, and through the press, that they had the right to organize and that therefore we couldn't argue that they didn't know that. Jean replied "bank employees are not going to be convinced by reading a leaflet. The fact is that no bank employees in English Canada have collective bargaining rights and until they do they're not going to believe that they can have them."

She went on to say "the legal precedent that most people are aware of, often in a distorted form, is the Bank of Nova Scotia Kitimat decision in 1959, and we have also discussed that in bulletins. We know, and bank employees know, that the bank's argument at that time was that the only appropriate bargaining unit was a national unit of all of their employees in the whole country. And many bank employees, along with many other people, were under the mistaken impression that the 1959 Kitimat decision had agreed with the bank's contention that the only appropriate bargaining unit was a national unit."

Typically underestimating us and all bank employees, the Bank's lawyer couldn't believe that we would have been affected by a CLRB decision. After all, the banks' employees are perfectly happy and not at all interested in unions. He expressed disbelief that bank workers had heard about the Kitimat decision. "And how would they, if they heard it, understand it?" he blustered indignantly. " Now would you please explain that to the Board. You're asking the Board to believe that the employees of this bank, because of a decision of the federal Board many years ago, decided that they didn't have the right to have a union. Do you expect the Board to accept that, Miss Rands?"

"I have met, personally, dozens of bank employees who have informed me that legally the banks can only be organized nationally," Jean replied. "I have also met a dozen or so bank employees who knew more specifically either that a bank in Kitimat had applied and been rejected or another distorted version of it, such as that bank in Nova Scotia had applied and been rejected on the grounds that only the whole country could be organized. That's the kind of feedback that I to some extent assume comes from the Kitimat decision. Okay?"

The bank's lawyer still couldn't believe it. "So you are asking the Board to believe that in your campaign for the last several months, starting last August, employees were so overwhelmed by the effect and impact of the Kitimat decision that they didn't think they could have a union. Is that right?"

"I'm saying that employees were so overwhelmed by the size and apparent power of the Canadian chartered banks, and by the fact that none of them have been organized, that they did not feel that they practically had the right to trade union representation."

"I'm mystified how so many people should know about a decision, a technical decision of the Board, made by the Board nineteen years ago. However."

"Well, you know, I worked in insurance for a long, long time, and I'll tell you that every time I worked in a place and talked about a union, I was told about someone who had talked about a union and been fired, five or ten or fifteen years previously. It's amazing the long memories that people have."

"Well yours seems to be like that of an elephant."

The bank's lawyer had a newspaper clipping quoting Jackie as saying that SORWUC was "prepared to tackle the banks on a province-wide basis". He asked whether Jean agreed with Jackie's statement. Jean said, "whatever this Board decides, bank employees are going to unionize. The success we've had so far demonstrates that. People are not going to be prepared to give up." There followed a long argument between the lawyers about whether or not Jean had agreed with Jackie's statement.

We were actually glad that the bank introduced this evidence. We couldn't disclaim the branch unit at these hearings because that would amount to withdrawing our applications for certification. But we did want the Board to consider geographic units as an alternative.

The scariest questions of all were the ones about our constitution. The constitution said that where a local existed, application for membership must be made to the Local. It was revealed through Jean's testimony that we had violated that section. Even after Local 2 was formed, bank workers joined as headquarters members of the National Union and it was the National Union that applied for certification in the banks.

As we expected, the bank did a great song and dance on this point. They said our applications should be dismissed without a hearing because SORWUC National had no members in the banks. Our whole campaign could be wiped out on a technicality! They tried to get Jean to say that people who joined before Local 2 was formed had been transferred into Local 2 and were therefore no longer members of the National; and people who joined after Local 2 was formed were signed up in violation of the constitution and therefore weren't members at all. Jean kept repeating firmly that members of SORWUC locals were automatically members of the National Union.

The other major issue was whether we had a majority in each branch, and whether the withdrawals and resignations from the union should be considered in determining whether we had a majority.

The Board had previously ruled that the majority would be determined as of the date of the application for certification. The withdrawals came much later and were therefore considered irrelevant. However, shortly before the hearings, the rules had been changed. The Federal Court of Appeal had overturned a CLRB decision to grant certification at CKOY radio station. The Court ruled that the Board must determine majority status as of the date that the Board made its decision on whether or not to grant certification. This meant that we would only be certified if we had maintained our majorities through months and months of delay. Supposedly, the Canada Labour Code guaranteed our right to organize, but when we tried to put it into practice all sorts of mysterious obstacles were thrown in the way.

We attempted to present our case that the withdrawals resulted from management interference and should be disregarded. The Board did not allow much evidence along these lines—after all, Jean was not a bank worker who had withdrawn from the union and anything she had to say on the subject would be hearsay. However, she did make the point that the Board's long delay was a problem in itself—most of the withdrawals had come months after we had applied for certification.

After the lawyers had finished with Jean, the Board members asked questions like: How many meetings did you hold in this campaign? How many leaflets were distributed? Is it really true that there are no paid officers of the union? How many union officers work full-time or part-time on a volunteer basis? They seemed surprised and impressed at the answers. Throughout Jean's testmony, we gave her support from the audience as best we could—winking, laughing, even (to the Chairman's annoyance) clapping once or twice.

Members of Local 1 were running back and forth between the union office and the hearings, looking for files and delivering messages. They took detailed minutes. Each evening during the hearings, the notes were summarized and typed up for the early morning meeting we held each day with our lawyer. Copies of these minutes and all the exhibits were sent to the Canadian Union of Bank Employees (CUBE) in Ontario to help them prepare for their hearings which would be immediately after ours. UBW members got together for supper every night to go over our notes, try to figure out who was winning, and ready ourselves for the next day. Working in the bank was never this much fun. Though we were exhausted each night, we felt competent and strong.

The bank's first witness took the stand the second morning. E.S. Duffield was senior vice-president of Human Resources and Administration. He had been with the Commerce for thirty-eight years. Duffield explained the structure of senior management in the bank. The bank's lawyer brought out evidence about the services Head Office supplied to branches (computers, etc.) and bank policy effected at the Head Office level. It was a great sedative. Things picked up when Ian began cross-examination. Duffield said that personnel policies were set at the Head Office level but were carried out at the discretion of branch managers. Hiring and firing is done on Manager's recommendations. Managers and Regional Office have the power to carry out general policies set by Head Office and make decisions on a day-to-day basis regarding personnel. This man from Commerce Court seemed terribly removed from the goings on in an ordinary bank branch. He knew where all the Commerce U.S. branches were and how many they had in Europe, but couldn't remember how many there were in the Yukon.

The bank's next witness was Philip Cotton, the vice president of personnel since 1976. He was the modern personnel man. He seemed determined not to admit to any shred of autonomy on the part of a branch. It appeared that absolutely every decision ever made in the Commerce was made in Toronto. He often contradicted what Duffield, his boss, had said. (Us bored spectators sent each other notes, some of which commented on the fact that God lived in Toronto. We also drew maps showing all of Canada as a small suburb of Toronto.)

Next was David Balmer, assistant director of the Canadian Bankers' Association. He explained the clearing systems for the banks and compared it with the system in the U.S. I won't go into it as elaborately as he did. He had tons of documents complete with flow charts. How the clearing system worked was quite interesting but the testimony was, to say the least, a little drawn out.

He stated that in Canada there was one common system for clearing cheques. The two basic clearing methods were a centralized exchange at the Bank of Canada points, and in more remote areas, local exchange between banks. When a bank exchanges another bank's item, two pieces of paper are passed. Net positions are calculated and reserves held in the Bank of Canada are then adjusted by transferring value from one bank to another. Balmer said the government was interested in developing a telex system which would require common procedures and restrict the autonomy of each branch using the system. Was the bank going to argue that the whole banking system was so closely interconnected that the only logical bargaining unit would be all the employees of all the banks in the whole country?

The next witness was Ronald White, assistant general manager, systems division, of the Commerce. His job was maintenance and development of computer systems. He gave impressive and boring details of how each system worked. The point seemed to be that branches were not autonomous and that all important functions took place in Toronto. Our lawyer brought out the fact that the bank relied on unionized companies to provide some computer servicing and courier services and the bank had managed to survive. There was a discussion of the implications of strikes, fires, floods and other acts of God on the Canadian banking system.

By now we were on Day Three. The bank had finished presenting their evidence about the bargaining unit question. There was more consultation between Board and lawyers. We had planned to present more evidence on the difficulty of organizing in the banks, specifically the anti-union acts of management in the Commerce. The banks argued

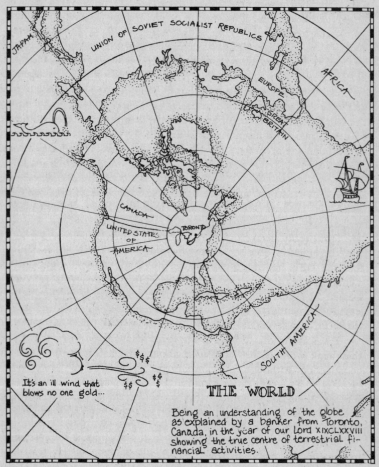

It's an ill wind that blows no one gold...

THE WORLD

Being an understanding of the globe as explained by a banker from Toronto, Canada, in the year of our Lord XIXCLXXVIII showing the true centre of terrestrial financial activities.

that this all had nothing to do with an appropriate bargaining unit. We argued that it did, because it had to do with difficulty in organizing. Clearly it had to do with determining the union's majority status. But as the bank's witnesses droned on and on, we realized that if we insisted on calling that evidence the hearing could not finish in the week that the Board had allotted. If the case was put over, it could be many months before we got a decision. We decided to drop everything else in return for an early ruling on the appropriate bargaining unit. We dropped the issue of the sudden transfer of Hooper and Wong to Victory Square and their subsequent anti-union activities. The case of Chris in Ganges who had been fired and then, on the union's intervention reinstated, was held over until July. The question of which positions within a branch should be included in the bargaining unit was also held over.

The Board announced that after lunch on Day Four the lawyers would begin their arguments on the appropriateness of the bargaining unit, whether the withdrawals should be accepted or disregarded by the Board, and whether SORWUC was a proper union.

That afternoon was supposed to start with Ian's argument. However, we weren't satisfied with our evidence on the constitutional problem. And the Board, in its remoteness, had not yet heard from a real live bank worker. We needed a witness from the UBW. We had originally planned to have Jackie testify about this and about anti-union activity at Victory Square. At the last minute, we realized that Ian didn't know the story of Jackie's job application at the Commerce. She had thought that the bank might discriminate against her for previous union activity, so although she accurately described her experience and qualifications, she had altered the specific jobs and employers in parts of her work history. This would surely be raised by the bank, her credibility as a witness could be affected, and the bank might try to use it as grounds for firing. Ian freaked out. Ian decided that I would testify instead. I freaked out.

I was really nervous. Mostly all I had to do was identify the notice and the minutes of our January membership meeting which showed that the UBW had discussed and approved the constitutional amendments and resolutions passed by the national convention. At first it seemed I might not even get to do that, since the bank's lawyer objected vehemently to such important evidence being introduced so late. However, it was determined that the Board would hear my evidence.

I was afraid that the bank's lawyers would try to use me to prove that bank workers were confused about what had happened with the constitution. Although I wasn't confused, it seemed likely that I would be after some cross-examination by the bank's lawyers. They did ask a few questions about quorums for meetings, and how long it takes for mail to be delivered in Vancouver, but I survived and (I'm told) didn't sound confused at all.

That was the last of the evidence. Now it was time for each lawyer to sum up his case. Ian went first on the question of the bargaining unit. He referred to banks in the U.S. which had been certified branch

by branch, as well as retail chains in the U.S. and Canada. He stressed
that to implement the law that said bank workers had the right to
unionize, the Board must establish a bargaining unit small enough
that it would be physically possible for a union to sign up a majority
of the employees. Again he raised the possibility of the province as a
unit, and argued that the Bank had deliberately downplayed the role of
the Regional Office by failing to call any of them as witnesses.

The bank's lawyer went on and on about how important banks are
to the economy and to each and every individual. "We are talking about
something that is very crucial to each and every person. We are talking
about that person's property rights. We are not talking about the conve-
nience of getting a service, whether it is transportation, whether it is
mailing a letter, whatever form it may be otherwise. We are talking
about your property rights, my property rights, and those of all Cana-
dians. We are talking about our right to deposit money and, more particularly, our right to withdraw it. And if that right is at all prejudiced,
my respectful submission is that confidence in our banking system,
upon which our whole fiscal structure is predicated, will be badly
undermined and seriously jeopardized."

He painted a terrifying picture of the effect of certifying branches
or even regions. "Now again I ask the Board to forget we are sitting in
this beautiful city and this beautiful province" (he was definitely uncomfortable being out of Toronto) "broaden our sights to the implications resulting from the chaos, the utter chaos that is inevitable if
the concept advanced by my friend is adopted by this honourable
board. ("My friend" was the union's lawyer! That's legal jargon.)

". . . There are in excess of seventy-five operating divisions among
the chartered banks. I ask the Board simply to test even that situation
against sequential bargaining, sequential strikes. The impact on our economy. The impact on our people. Chaos is probably inadequate to de-
scribe the consequences of my friend's proposition within the magni-
tude of this situation and these figures."

According to the bank's lawyer, the evidence showed "a uni-
system of banking, controlled in all aspects centrally, at the Head
Office . . . . The branch is not a profit centre. It is not an independent
unit. . . . Even grievances cannot be settled within the branch."

He made an impassioned plea for industry-wide bargaining (interesting in view of the position the banks later adopted in response to such
proposals from us). "The advantages of this sort of centralized bargaining to labour, management and government, as well as to the public,
are obvious to the public themselves. . . . How conceivably can an
agreement be negotiated in these circumstances on the basis of a unit
of the nature or natures proposed by the applicant? Further, I ask the
Board to consider and place itself in both the union's position and
management's position in the terms of the logistics, the costs, the
difficulties attendant upon the very negotiation of a multiplicity of
agreements; the difficulties of administration, the costs of administration to the parties, not management alone, the union as well, the
administration of a multiplicity of units, of separate unit agreements.

. . . We are not talking about five or six units ranging from four to twenty. We are talking about potentially 7,000. We are talking about, potentially, 1700 in this bank alone. It is a monster. My friend's client would create a monster. . . . Think in terms of the difficulties if not the impossibility of turning a monster around after it has taken off on a multi-unit, multi-agreement, sequential strike work stoppage tangent."

He argued that branch by branch certification "would introduce horrendous implications . . . multiple unions, multiple units, spread across the country, hither and yon, beyond control." Apparently still not grasping the fact that banks are subject to the labour law and the orders of the CLRB, he told the Board, "you should not ask of a bank that it indulge in that kind of experiment."

He concluded by saying that "a national unit alone would be appropriate in all the circumstances."

Ian then had an opportunity to answer the bank. He was neither quite so passionate nor quite so unreasonable. "If you determine, with the greatest respect, that only a national unit is appropriate, you are, in effect, legislating. You are taking over a function that ought and does belong only to Parliament. For to make a determination of such a wide-sweeping and confining nature would be to make the Canada Labour Code as it relates to a huge number of employees essentially inoperative."

He said the union too would favour joint bargaining and consolidating bargaining units. "The union has no intention of standing still. It does not propose to hold on to one or two or however many branches it may obtain on certification applications. It wants to expand and to consolidate. The objectives are clear. It's in everyone's interest to try and get the largest bargaining unit possible." He stressed again that the Board could choose from a whole range of appropriate bargaining units, from the branch to the province.

We all went back to work in the banks, feeling frustrated that we hadn't been allowed to tell the Board about the outrageous activities of Hooper and Wong and other aspects of the anti-union campaign. But we felt that we done a good job of putting forward our case. Now, we had to wait for the Board's decision.

The Board members went back to Ontario to hear the CUBE applications for four bank branches near London, Ontario. They were to return to B.C. in July to hear evidence about who should be excluded from the bargaining unit, and about unfair labour practices.

The next two months seemed an eternity. We tried to prepare ourselves for any eventuality, and spent a lot of time speculating as to what the Board's ruling might be. Most bank workers seemed to be waiting for the Board to decide whether the branch was a unit and whether SORWUC was a union before they would join.

On June 14, 1977 we received the decision. The Board ruled that each branch was an appropriate bargaining unit. I remember being in the vault at work, giving the Loomis men the money parcels for the week. Also in the vault were a couple of supervisors, both active in the anti-union campaign. Jackie came running into the vault yelling "We won! It's branch by branch!" I moaned, "Oh no! It can't be!" The supervisors moaned the same thing.

The Board had dismissed the bank's horror stories as follows: "We have decided that the single branch location of the Commerce encompasses employees with a community of interest and is an appropriate bargaining unit . . . The counter arguments of the employer are in large measure hypothetical fears that we find should not prevail over the tangible realities of the union's position."

We were jubilant that we had won, but also surprised and apprehensive. Would we really be able to organize branch by branch?

The days following the decision convinced us all that it was a great victory. The press was plastered with it. The union office was nutso. The phones rang all day long. It was so big and meant so much to so many bank workers and we had done it! We had done what everyone said was impossible. We were smug and self-righteous to the BIG members at Victory Square, and for the first time in months it was us who could gloat all over them.

Our organizing drive was booming, and we realized this was just the beginning. Although we still had to go through the July hearing, we knew we would be certified at some branches. We had to prepare for negotiations, and to be successful in negotiations we had to increase our organizing activity. We wrote the CLC in Ottawa, reported on our campaign and the decision, and asked for financial support. They replied that they would discuss it at their next meeting. That was the last we heard about that appeal, but donations from local unions affiliated to the CLC increased considerably following the Board's decision. At last everyone knew that it was possible to organize the banks.

Just before the decision, SORWUC signed its first contract in the finance industry. The employees at the Electrical Trades Credit Union had to take a strike vote and convince management they were prepared to act on it, but at last—six months after we were certified there— we had signed an excellent contract. The starting rate went from $600 per month to $875 per month for a thirty-three hour work week. We won improved vacations, job security, benefits for part-time employees and time off for union meetings. It was a great contract, and great timing for bank workers. The work of the credit union workers in writing up proposals and negotiating with their employer, made a big contribution to the preparation for negotiations in the banks.

We have learned so much about union
You can't win a war if you're on your own
You've got to have friends who will walk beside you
Together we can win where we can't alone.
— A new version of Holly Near's "Hang in There"

7   They'll Promise Us Anything

Just before the July hearings the full implications of the CKOY decision began to sink in. People at the CLRB offices kept talking about "CKOY" and our lawyer kept telling us to remember "CKOY". It meant that whether we had majorities in the branches, or whether we were in a vote situation would be determined as of the date of the July hearings. Therefore the petitions, letters of withdrawals and protests would be taken into consideration. This meant some applications could be rejected without even a vote where our membership had fallen below thirty-five per cent.

In response to the Court's decision about CKOY, the CLRB amended its regulations in March. When deciding whether a union had a majority in a bargaining unit, the Board would now disregard resignations from the union unless they were mailed within ten days following notice of the application for certification. The union would get copies of all correspondence, including the names of people who signed the petitions and letters. Previously people had been able to register opposition to the union anonymously. Now they would have to answer to their co-workers, and could be summonsed by the union to appear at a hearing. The union argued that these regulations should be applied retroactively to cover our applications. The Board ruled against us; they would consider resignations in determining whether the union had a majority in branches we had applied for before the regulations were changed.

It was our contention that if the Board was going to consider withdrawals they must also consider new memberships. Even if a branch had applied with less than a majority, if we could sign up a majority in the branch before the hearing then we should be certified without a vote.

The union office became even more frantic. Some of the branches were very close to majorities. We needed to make sure not only that members' dues were paid up-to-date, but that copies of all receipts were available for the CLRB. We were madly rushing around, not only signing up new branches but trying to sign up all the new employees in old branches.

The hearings were held July 7 to 14 and were to determine who would be excluded from the bargaining units and whether or not we had a majority in each branch. We had twenty-two applications before the Board by this time, having applied for another two since the first hearing. Different banks argued the exclusion of secretaries, stenos and dicta-typists, loans officers, part-time employees, branch officers in-training, teller trainees and management trainees. The Board decided that only management trainees should be excluded. (Even though it was practically unheard of for the Court to overturn such technical decisions by the Board, the banks appealed the decisions on exclusions. The appeals were dismissed by the Court, but they did have the effect of diverting time, energy and money from organizing). The Board ruled that we had majorities in five branches and certified us for those. Votes were ordered in seventeen, even though we had a majority in some of them. Thirteen new applications were made between June and September, 1977 when the votes were counted, including two in Saskatchewan.

During our campaign for the votes, it was too tense to hold meetings so we wrote or called people at home. Union supporters gave us the names and addresses or phone numbers of employees who might be convinced to vote for the union. One of the problems was that the union people in the branches were too scared to do the arguing themselves. The anti-union employees were also phoning people at home. Taking a coffee break in those days was a nerve-wracking ordeal. There was no telling what vicious nasty argument would be going on in the staff room. Branch managers were holding meetings telling us that our wages and benefits would probably be frozen if we were certified, and in addition to the banks' rules we would be subject to union rules and regulations, and we would have to start punching a time clock. Of course, the banks' customers weren't going to be left out either. Customers would tell us how proud they were to be dealing with a union branch, that we deserved better wages and they were pleased that we were finally standing up for ourselves. There were also the million dollar accounts who threatened to pull out of the branch if the union won. We were feeling quite battered.

The votes were held in early August. The ballot box was set up in the staff lounge, coffee room or conference room in each branch. We had to find people to scrutinize votes all over the province. The branch managers scrutinized for the bank.

From August 3 to August 25, seventeen votes were held. We lost fourteen. Our press statement said we were not surprised; we had expected to lose those votes because of the length of time that had elapsed between the application date and the date of the vote. There was a short article in the paper saying "Fledgling Union Flounders". At the time we were announcing a new application for certification every week and we were still exclaiming about our victory in the branch-by-branch decision so the press did not dwell on the vote losses.

Of the Commerce branches, we were automatically certified for Port McNeill and votes were ordered in seven others. As the anti-union employees were most active in the Commerce, we thought we'd lose them all. We won one at the Ganges branch. Everyone there had been so secretive about how they were going to vote in order to avoid harassment that when we called the branch to offer congratulations we had no idea who to ask for! At the Port Hardy branch the vote was tied four to four—this was counted as a loss, as exactly fifty per cent is not a majority. At Victory Square, the vote was seventeen to two against the union. Dodie and Jackie in a fit of sarcasm kept asking everyone who had voted in favour of the union.

We lost the vote in our only application for a TD branch.

To this day we have no idea why the Board ordered votes at our Scotia branches. The Board has the power to make such arbitrary decisions and we never got a good explanation for it. We had applied with majorities at all and their dues were paid up. We lost one of the votes in the branches and we got clobbered in the vote at the Scotia Data Centre.

We had applied with less than a majority at the Scotia Data Centre and never managed to build an organization. The months waiting for the certification vote had been difficult. Management had wasted no time in starting their anti-union campaign and carried it on until the vote. An assistant supervisor had called a meeting in the lunch room and told the other employees that she was being transferred to Toronto so it didn't concern her but it was her opinion that they did not need a union and shouldn't join the UBW. An administration officer had waited for employees in the parking lot and approached them with a petition. One employee said that she read it, but it was a lot of legal gobbledy gook to her so she asked the administration officer what it meant. The administration officer said if she was having second thoughts about joining the union she should sign the petition. The employee said she knew her own mind and walked away but unfortunately that wasn't true of most of the employees. (This employee quit because of illness in the family and when she reapplied she could not get back on. She has ten years experience.)

Some employees had been invited to attend a meeting which they were led to believe was a pro and con meeting with just Data Centre employees. It was held at a restaurant and conducting the meeting was the administration officer and Bonnie Wong. Wong said that the UBW was $100,000 in debt and only wanted their membership fees to pay off this debt. She said she couldn't sleep at night because she was being threatened and her car was being followed and someone was trying to kill her. This sounded like something out of "The Godfather", but to the bank workers who knew nothing about unions it was frightening.

The week before the certification vote, management had informed employees that they would be receiving a fifteen cents per hour increase, a regular coffee break and no more overtime. They had earlier received the dental plan and sick pay. The employees would be paid sick pay if they were sick on their scheduled night. The vote was seventy-two to twenty against the union.

Immediately after the vote, management told employees that the coffee break wouldn't work out because it would conflict with the Loomis pickup and computer time. They were also told that the fifteen cents per hour increase was only if their production increased. As for no more overtime, the day after the votes were counted we were once again required to work involuntary overtime. So much for verbal promises and no union.

There were several members of BIG at the Data Centre. They did not restrict their activities to the Data Centre. One of them phoned the Scotia branch in Haney, a small town about sixty-five kilometres east of Vancouver, to tell the employees that should they "go union" the Data Centre was already preparing to shut down the branch. The women in Haney were terrified for their jobs. Still, it was hard to believe that people who had been so strong for so long would believe the anti-union propaganda and vote against the union. We lost the vote at Haney and won at the Vancouver Heights and SFU branches of the Scotia.

We were automatically certified at four Bank of Montreal branches and votes were conducted in the other five. These votes were the most upsetting because they were so close. At the Main and Hastings branch in Vancouver it was ten to nine against the union, at Cloverdale thirteen to twelve against and at Main Branch in Nanaimo eighteen to eighteen. We knew how closely divided the branches were but we had hoped the scales would tip our way. We were never again so naive. Luck has nothing to do with winning.

Although the votes were held over a three week period they were all counted on September 1 and 2 at the Board offices.

That Friday evening several of us ended up drinking in a lounge on the North Shore. Union supporters came to console us. There were Dodie and Jackie being analytical and academic while they explained why we had lost all those votes. Really, it made sense—the wait, the intimidation, the turn-over. Of course we would lose all those votes. In some branches we had been strong as individuals but we had not acted collectively. We weren't used to working together. In those branches where we were able to act collectively the union majority had been retained. In the Port McNeill, Port Alberni and Regina branches, we had acted like a union from the beginning—even without a contract. We had elected a shop steward immediately, told the manager who she was and as things came up about our jobs or the union, management had to deal with our representatives who spoke for the collective. Also in these branches, encouragement and moral support from other trade unionists helped people in the struggle. Since the branch-by-branch decision, there was a new strategy. We would only apply for those branches where a majority had signed up into the union. We had applied for ten more branches since the decision on the bargaining unit. We knew the rules now. There should be few losses now. It all made sense. Then how come we felt so overwhelmed?

I saw the banks' own tellers
Working hard for small return
While the bankers get more profits
That they never toiled to earn.
— An additional verse to "Banks are
Made of Marble", traditional labour song

8   Organizing the Sunshine Coast

Following the CLRB decisions in the summer of 1977 there was a burst of organizing. Now, we said, the question of a union in the banks is no longer a matter for the Board but for the bank workers themselves. Hundreds of bank workers responded.

On the Sechelt Peninsula, we signed up a majority in three of the seven bank branches and came close in a fourth. Events on the Peninsula over the next year were like a microcosm of the bank organizing campaign as a whole. Bank management in this area tried every possible means to defeat the union. Union members, with strong community support, put up a great fight.

The Peninsula, with a population of about 14,000, is a rural/industrial/tourist area which can only be reached from Vancouver by water. The major industries are the pulp mill, fishing and logging. The CPU, the IWA, the UFAWU and the B.C. Ferry and Marine Workers Union are all strong.

Our first application for certification was on July 5, 1977 for employees of the Royal Bank in Sechelt. This application received the usual attention from the bank's Regional Office. Two personnel officers came to the branch to meet with employees. They asked for questions, asked to hear about any problems, and told employees to contact them in Vancouver if there were any problems.

At the time we were signing up members on the Peninsula, OTEU, the B.C. name of the Office and Professional Employees International Union mailed leaflets to bank branches in B.C. The OTEU is the CLC affiliate which, according to the CLC, had the "jurisdiction" to organize banks. (One of the objectives of the CLC is "to define the organizing jurisdiction of the affiliates", that is, the industry or occupation which each affiliate union is to organize. The CLC attempts to protect the jurisdiction of each affiliate against other affiliates and against independent unions who aren't bound by the CLC's division of jurisdiction. The CLC constitution says: "It shall be the responsibility of the officers, affiliates and chartered bodies of this Congress to actively encourage the elimination of conflict and duplicating organizations of jurisdiction through agreement, merger and other means.") But once the UBW got started, the OTEU demanded that the CLC affiliates support them rather than SORWUC because "we've had a jurisdiction to organize banks for forty years"! It may be that in most branches the OTEU leaflets were filed by management in the garbage without being seen by bank employees. But in the Royal branches at Sechelt and

Gibsons, and in the Gibsons branch of the Bank of Montreal, management used this leaflet to their own advantage. At one branch, the leaflet
was circulated by management for all employees to initial, hardly the
usual response to union literature! At another branch, the accountant
passed the leaflet around and urged employees to investigate the OTEU
before deciding which union to join. This approach was successful at
the Royal in Sechelt. All but one employee signed a letter resigning
from the union. The one exception was the main union organizer in
the branch who had gone on vacation right after the application for
certification was submitted. (Bad timing!) We were forced to withdraw this application. Management's communications were so good by
this time that our members in the Royal in Gibsons were informed that
the Royal in Sechelt had withdrawn from the union before it even
happened! We never did get a majority at the Bank of Montreal.

Applications for certification for employees of the Commerce and
the Royal in Gibsons went to the Board on July 13, 1977. The Gibsons
branch of the Commerce is in a shopping mall so it's open on Saturdays
and closed on Mondays. There were five employees plus the manager
and an accountant when we applied for certification. Four out of the
five joined the union. They had decided to organize for basically the
same reasons bank workers all over the province were joining the union:
they felt they were skilled workers and terribly underpaid. The staff in
this branch socialized with each other after business hours and got
along well with their manager. They recognized that he was powerless
to change the basic working conditions and benefits which were established by Regional Office or Head Office. Other working people on the
Peninsula made twice as much money as they did and they knew that
people had fought for and won those rights and conditions by joining
together in unions. Obviously, that was what was needed in the banks.

On Wednesday, July 13, the union office called the branch and
told the accountant that the union had applied for certification that
day. The manager was called back from his vacation. He arrived in the
branch Thursday morning, stayed briefly and then went to Regional
Office in Vancouver.

On Friday afternoon, the manager and the accountant spoke to
employees individually. The manager told employees that he felt sick
about the fact that they had joined the union, that they should have
talked to him about it, and that he hadn't been able to sleep since it
happened. The accountant said that the manager's career was over.

On Saturday morning at 9:30 a.m., the manager called the employees in to the coffee room for a meeting. He said he had decided
that if the bank wouldn't transfer him, he would resign. He would
apply for a transfer, but he didn't think the bank would transfer him.
The only employee who hadn't joined the union asked if there was
anything they could do to get him to stay. The manager said there was
nothing anyone could do. The manager and two employees were in
tears. Two employees were thinking of quitting the branch. Everyone
felt terribly guilty for destroying the manager's vacation and probably
his whole career.

At the time we thought the manager had unfortunately taken the whole thing personally, and was particularly upset because he had been called back from vacation. We did not think that it was part of a strategy for dealing with the union. It was much later that we read this report of a rumour in the Financial Post:

> CONFIRM OR DENY: That Canada's major chartered banks have held talks with a professional labor fighter from Chicago who is advising them on methods to help stave off unionization of their 140,000 employees.
>
> On another front, some bank managers apparently have been given "canned" speeches to their present staffs, complete with "built-in" pauses where the managers are supposed to get emotional.

We considered filing an unfair labour practice complaint about the meeting. We decided it would be more useful to put our energy into providing information and support to our Gibsons members so that we could maintain our majority in each branch through the crucial ten-day period. (According to the CLRB regulations, employees who withdrew from the union within ten days of the posting of the notice of certification application, would not be counted as members. That meant the bank and/or anti-union employees had ten days in which to campaign to convince people to quit the union. If they were successful, the union would lose majority support and be forced to withdraw the application for certification.)

We had some great meetings in Gibsons. At one meeting, the accountants from both the Royal and the Commerce were there as well as a "senior loans officer" (the Royal's name for an assistant manager), along with most of the members of the bargaining units in the branches where we had applied. Practically all the anti-union arguments imaginable were raised at this meeting and answered by the Gibsons union members and a SORWUC rep from Vancouver.

Everyone was given copies of various leaflets, a report on the July hearings regarding exclusions, copies of the union constitution, and copies of the contract between SORWUC and the Electrical Trades Credit Union. One of the employees presented a list of written questions which set off a great discussion.

The way some of the questions were presented made them sound more like a test than a request for information, but they raised a lot of important issues. One problem was bank workers seeing the union as an outside entity that would do things for them, rather than an organization of bank workers doing things for themselves. There was the problem of transfers and transferability of seniority, which we later had a hard time dealing with in negotiations on a branch-by-branch basis. Some bank workers feared they would lose more than they would gain, i.e. they wouldn't be able to go home early when their work was done; they wouldn't get any more wages because of the AIB; they might lose other benefits. The questions also reflected a suspicion of unions—we were accused, for instance, of paying union leaders both too much and too little all in the same breath.

We did withstand the ten days. At the Commerce branch the manager had not been transferred, and had not resigned. Neither had any of the employees. We were certified on August 16. In the Royal the anti-union campaign continued. A number of non-union employees wrote to the Board expressing opposition to the union and asking for a vote.

Certification at the Royal was delayed by legal hassles. Once the Board had made its decision that a branch was an appropriate bargaining unit, we were confident there would be no more long waits for certification. When we applied for the Royal in Gibsons, the bank's reply said they did not agree that the branch was an appropriate unit but they were not about to argue the point. However, on August 10, they did. The bank wrote to the Board and said they had new evidence on the question of the branch as the bargaining unit. The new evidence was a clipping from the Montreal Gazette datelined Toronto which quoted Jackie Ainsworth in Vancouver to the effect that the union was asking for joint bargaining in the banks. The banks produced this as evidence that even the union didn't think the branch was an appropriate unit. Although the Board had originally decided not to hold a hearing about the Gibsons certification, the Royal Bank insisted. The largest chartered bank in Canada was not prepared to accept union certification without its own "day in court".

The hearing on the Gibsons application was held October 18, 19 and 20, 1977 in Vancouver. We expected the decision would apply to the branches in Kamloops and in Melfort, Saskatchewan. Two union members from the Royal in Gibsons had time off work to attend the hearings.

Unlike the other banks who had asked the Board to establish a Canada-wide bargaining unit, the Royal asked for a regional unit. They also argued that the stenographer and the personal loans officer should be excluded from the unit, and that the application should be rejected because a majority of employees in Gibsons did not support the union.

The personal loans officer in the branch appeared at the hearing representing the five employees who had signed the letter opposing the application for certification. She argued that personal loans officers had little in common with clerical employees in the branch and that she should not be included in the bargaining unit. The Board asked how then could she represent the other employees opposed to the union if they had so little in common, whereupon she admitted that she had a common interest in benefits. She also argued that a majority of employees did not support the union although only a minority had signed the letter. She claimed that people had joined the union because of misinformation and that the union had befogged people's minds because wine had been served at a meeting.

The Board's decision came down on November 3, 1977, almost four months after the union had applied for certification. We had won, a victory diluted by the time taken to achieve it.

Well I'm tired of working my life away
And giving somebody else all of my pay
While they get rich on the profits that I lose
And leaving me here with the working girl blues.
— "Working Girl Blues" by
Hazel Dickens and Alice Gerrard

9   Saskatchewan

Two tellers in the Royal Bank in Melfort, Saskatchewan, about 240 kilometres north-east of Saskatoon, got together in early 1977 to try to do something about wages and conditions in their branch. Their wages were barely enough to cover basic living expenses. The starting wage in banks was often the minimum required by the Federal law, which was lower than the Saskatchewan provincial minimum wage! One of the tellers had been promised a certain starting wage and turned down another job to work at the branch only to find that her first pay cheque was significantly smaller than promised. Her complaints were ignored. Promised holidays would be denied at the last minute for arbitrary reasons. Deductions were made from pay cheques to pay for soda pop in the coffee room without the employees' permission. The manager was unapproachable and uninterested. The tellers had gone over his head to Regional Office to demand an investigation. Regional Office promised action and did nothing.

The two tellers began meeting with other women in their branch to discuss some kind of action. They met in secret, changing homes each time to be less obvious in the small community. After a few months of sharing concerns, they decided that to unionize was the only answer.

A friend in Regina, who had heard of SORWUC through the media and through friends, told the Melfort bank workers about it. They wrote to SORWUC for information and studied the material closely when it arrived. They then wrote again and said they were really interested and wanted to talk to someone from the union.

About this time the Saskatchewan Federation of Labour organized a conference for women trade unionists, and invited a speaker from SORWUC in Vancouver. This was an opportunity to meet with other trade unionists about support for the Melfort bank workers. If the people in Melfort joined the UBW there would have to be an independent organization formed in Saskatchewan. The Vancouver office had neither the time nor the money to organize and negotiate in another province. Women at the conference encouraged SORWUC to begin a campaign in Saskatchewan.

Saskatchewan has a history of struggle within the CLC to put the rights and interests of workers in Saskatchewan ahead of decisions by CLC leaders and national office leaders in Ontario. CUPE, the Grain Services Union and Retail, Wholesale and Department Store Union (RWDSU) had on occasion formed a dissident alliance within the

Saskatchewan Federation of Labour. Organizing the unorganized was part of their program. RWDSU had broken away from the international in 1971 and succeeded in building a strong Saskatchewan union. Because of this, the CLC expelled RWDSU but RWDSU's alliances with other unions continued, giving it a unique position of solidarity with the CLC affiliated unions as well as independence from CLC directives. RWDSU was actively organizing service, retail and restaurant workers.

In 1976 RWDSU had renewed its drive to organize the credit unions. Credit unions are more numerous in Saskatchewan than any other province except Quebec, and represent a significant portion of the finance industry. This organizing drive was only partly successful, with certifications in Saskatoon and Yorkton. As part of their anti-union campaign, the credit unions raised wages in non-union branches, putting bank wages behind those of credit unions. Bank management was meeting all across the province to figure out ways to prevent union interest among their workers without having to raise wages to the credit union levels. The credit unions and banks are located side by side in almost every city, town and village in the province. Bank workers began meeting to compare wages.

Melfort was one town in which the Royal Bank employees compared their wages and found that they were paid less than their friends in the credit unions and even in other Royal branches. Their initial interest in unionizing was what was needed to bring together a number of support groups and individuals in the province.

Jean Burgess had been working for the RWDSU on the credit union drive. She met with the SORWUC rep at the conference in Saskatoon and then visited the Vancouver office. She agreed to investigate the possibility of setting up a support organization for SORWUC in Saskatchewan. Her first step was to meet with the bank workers in Melfort. Burgess describes that meeting in August 1977 as very exciting:

> Six women from the branch attended. They told me what they wanted and I told them everything I knew about SORWUC. They were not only ready to sign union cards but to become active in setting up the union. They planned another meeting for the following week and invited other employees from the branch. I don't think any of us knew what we were getting into as far as demands on time and energy were concerned. We were all pretty nervous about our ability to do what had to be done. But we did know that if things were ever going to improve, we had to do it ourselves.

Events moved quickly after this. In August 1977 SORWUC National sent Jean Rands to Saskatchewan for a week to help set up supporting committees in Saskatoon and Regina. Jean Burgess was to coordinate the provincial campaign with the objective of laying the base for a bank workers' union. Others in the committees took on various tasks, from organizing leafletting to fund-raising. The committee members from both cities had a wide range of experience. A few were active union members, others were working in non-union jobs, some were feminists, some were students and a few had previously worked as bank tellers. The committee members saw themselves as supporters of the union, not as its decision-makers.

Rands and Burgess met with representatives of RWDSU, CUPE, Grain Services Union, the IWA, and the Saskatchewan Federation of Labour and found a lot of support for SORWUC's campaign in the banks. RWDSU later provided the UBW with a phone in their office. Gail Powell, who worked there, was active in organizing bank workers in Regina and helping us with grievances and negotiations. The meeting with the rep of the Office and Professional Employees International Union was brief and unfriendly. The OPEIU was not prepared to organize bank workers in Saskatchewan; it was prepared, however, to oppose such efforts by SORWUC. This was a hint of what was to follow with regard to CLC opposition.

A majority of the employees at the Royal's Melfort branch joined the union and on August 26, 1977 SORWUC applied for certification. The Saskatchewan UBW drive was underway.

While the Melfort members anxiously waited for the notice of their application to be received by the bank, the organizing campaign was set in motion in Regina and Saskatoon. A mass leafletting of each branch in each city was undertaken. In Regina there was an immediate response. A meeting of workers at the Scotia Main branch was arranged and within a week of hard organizing work a majority had signed union cards. The union applied for certification for this second branch, the first main branch in the country, on September 2, 1977. Both committees received many calls from bank workers; interest was high. Union membership increased, but we were not able to sign up a majority in any other branch.

Union locals were informed of our activities. We asked them for both moral and financial support. Similar appeals were sent to selected organizations such as women's groups. We organized fund-raising teas and a benefit to reach potential supporters. A newsletter was sent out on an occasional basis throughout the next two years, informing friends and supporters of SORWUC's activities, and we did regular press releases. We were approached by unorganized workers from workplaces other than banks; these contacts were referred to other unions.

In October a second leafletting of each branch in each city was undertaken. This led to the intervention of the United Steelworkers in the organizing drive in Saskatoon.

This was a shocking and discouraging experience for the supporting committee. Although by this time it had become quite clear that CLC support would not be forthcoming, the extent and nature of its opposition was a blow to the organizers. A SORWUC volunteer had been invited by a bank worker at the Confederation Park branch of the TD to speak to a group of interested workers. The meeting went well, but sign-ups were to take place at a second larger meeting. A Steelworkers' rep learned of the meeting and talked to them about it. He slandered and misrepresented SORWUC. The workers joined the United Steelworkers of America and they were later certified. The Steelworkers rep admitted his reason for doing this was only to stop SORWUC from unionizing the branch, and that the Steelworkers were not interested in representing bank workers. The CLC rep for the region confirmed that the CLC would continue to campaign against SORWUC.

This setback was eclipsed however by the application for certification of the TD Main Branch in Regina. In our first two months the supporting committees had filed three applications for certification with the CLRB, signed up thirty or so other bank workers, leafletted forty banks, developed support groups and raised $5000 from unions and individuals.

It was hard to tell the difference between anti-union activity and regular oppressive conditions in the branches. Bank workers had lived and worked under these conditions for quite a while and we couldn't suddenly fight back on all issues. Initially we were prepared to oppose what was seen as anti-union, but we were unsure about opposing ordinary unfair degrading management decisions. Management had always claimed the right to decide everything. Each unfair decision imposed upon the workers reinforced total management power and undermined the legitimacy of the union.

In Melfort, the manager called "the girls" into his office one by one, closed the door, and criticized them for having anything to do with the union. Some of the women remained silent and laughed about it afterwards. Others signed a management-initiated letter to the CLRB saying there was disagreement in the branch about unionizing and asking that a vote be held.

Job descriptions were changed causing suspicion and concern. New staff were hired at higher wages and it was suspected that management was trying to wipe out the union's majority. A junior teller was promoted into a new position that would normally have gone to one of the more active union members. This created conflict between the women until at a union meeting it was recognized as a "divide and conquer" tactic.

Management would be extra friendly one day and rude and abrupt the next. This created an atmosphere of uncertainty and insecurity. Rumours were circulated about possible firings, holding back the regular wage increase, closing down the branch and a trained "scab" staff at Regional Office. Holidays were refused at the requested time; overtime would be ordered at the last minute. Job evaluation time was interesting —the best worker at Melfort, who also supported the union, was suddenly given a poor evaluation.

In Regina, the Scotia and TD managements carried out similar tactics; tactics common to many other anti-union establishments. In late September, the Scotia was the scene of an internal campaign against the union.

FELLOW SCOTIABANKERS

As you are aware our Branch was recently approached by the United Bank Workers Local #2 of the Service, Office and Retail Workers Union of Canada to form a union within our office. NOW is the time we should be asking ourselves some serious questions, such as:

Do we really want a union?

If we DO want a union, is SORWUC the right one for us?

What can SORWUC **really** do for us?

Only you can answer the first question, but once we vote a union in, it will be very difficult to change our minds if we are not satisfied.

SORWUC implies that they will be able to negotiate increases beyond A.I.B. guidelines. Let them prove it before we buy it! Do you **really** think, that in the face of union pressure, the Bank is not giving the maximum increases possible under A.I.B.? Do you think that the Bank will pay higher wages to a Branch represented by SORWUC than to one which is not? NONSENSE!!

SORWUC claims they can improve working conditions. How? Are our working conditions so bad? We know there is always room for some improvement, but do we need a union to do it for us? Can SORWUC negotiate job satisfaction? Can they negotiate pleasant employee/management relationships? Can they guarantee that we won't lose the good things that we have now? Let's face it, money isn't everything, and SORWUC hasn't even proven they can deliver that.

What will we gain if we're forced out on strike? NOTHING!! What do we have to lose by waiting? Again, nothing! Once we see if SORWUC can fulfill all of their promises, then we should decide, not now.

LET'S NOT MAKE A DECISION THAT WE WILL LIVE TO REGRET!

We LIKE our jobs. We don't need representation. We are strong as individuals, and as individuals WE CAN SPEAK FOR OURSELVES!

HAPPY TO BE A NON-UNION BANKER!

D. Ripplinger

This campaign caused some union members to withdraw from the union. Because of the withdrawals, the CLRB ordered a vote to take place at the Scotia on November 25. Union members and volunteers fought hard to win this vote; they contacted other workers through the mail and at home to talk about the union. No further support was lost but no more was gained and we lost the vote twenty-two to eighteen. Like in B.C., the employees were being cautious and taking a "wait and see" attitude. In October, the bank had granted all their Saskatchewan employees three weeks vacation with pay, a benefit already enjoyed by workers covered by Saskatchewan provincial labour law. This new benefit on the one hand, and their threat of freezing wages on the other, reinforced the employees' cautious attitudes. Finally, the three month wait between the application and the vote made it difficult to sustain the momentum of the union and allowed management a lot of time to plant fears among the employees.

The TD management was much less smooth in their approach. Gloria Kups, a union member who had held one of the first organizing meetings at her home, was put on probation and unfavourable remarks were placed on her file. She had worked at the branch for four years and her work had never before received an unfavourable mention. Other employees were taken in pairs by the manager to the Assiniboine Club, an elite Regina club, where they were asked to discuss the union. No one obliged. The union's majority held, and the branch was certified on December 20, 1977.

By the end of 1977, the UBW Saskatchewan had two certified branches, one in Regina and one in Melfort. In both branches, morale boosting was especially important because of harassment on the job. At the TD tension was high and union members were watched and criticized in their work. Two tellers quit their jobs because of this atmosphere; another was fired for a mistake which would normally have been accepted as part of the learning process. The union's chief steward, Barb Gaura, was treated rudely by her supervisors and criticized for procedures which in her six years at the branch had never before been commented on. The union tried to counteract such measures as best we could. Members would discuss the situation to build up morale; whenever possible the chief steward went in with members called to see management; lawyers notified the bank that their activities were illegal. Finally the union went public and filed four unfair labour practice complaints, held two public leaflettings of the branch and did a mailing to supporters describing the bank's activities. This caused one union, the Saskatchewan Union of Nurses, to threaten to withdraw their account from the branch because of the anti-union activity.

Our two certified branches were 240 kilometres apart and getting together was very difficult during the prairie winter. The different conditions of a branch in a small rural town and a large main branch in the city brought about some initial differences in contract proposals. We held provincial bargaining workshops so that all members and supporters could get together. We invited members of other unions to the workshops so that we could learn from their experiences at the bargaining table and in fighting anti-union activity. We also raised money to send bank workers to B.C. for the SORWUC National Convention and the UBW (B.C.) conferences.

By January 1978, we had our proposals together and gave "notice to bargain" to the banks. Bank workers were ready to start negotiating and we were also ready to establish a formal organization of bank workers in Saskatchewan. In February 1978 the Saskatchewan union members applied to the National Executive in B.C. for a charter for the UBW, Saskatchewan Section.

To carry on negotiations with two banks in Saskatchewan, a full-time worker was necessary. In March, Lynette Polson, a Vancouver bank worker, was hired for six months as the union's representative. Her salary was $800 per month. Lynette's job was mainly to coordinate negotiations. Jean Burgess in Melfort and Gail Powell in Regina continued to take a significant part in negotiations.

The hiring of a paid worker meant another appeal for funds from the community. Support continued from both unions and individuals. Especially generous was the RWDSU which donated approximately $3,000, as well as being flexible with regard to Gail Powell's activities with SORWUC. Also providing support were locals of CUPE, Grain Services Union, CUPW, IWA and other unions, as well as many individuals. A women's conference of the Saskatchewan Federation of Labour voted support for SORWUC. All these pledges did much to encourage members and volunteers alike.

We're fighting for a contract
We're fighting to be free—
This battle is a long one
There's room for you and me.
     — Additional verse to Florence Reese's
     "Which Side Are You On?"

10   A Living Wage

By the late summer of 1977 the UBW B.C. Section was ready to begin work on a contract. We were faced with such basic structural decisions as the formation of a contract committee, and how, with our scattered membership, we could ensure involvement by all. What would be the role of members in non-certified branches? Who would handle the negotiations? With different job descriptions, personnel policies and wages in each bank, how could we come up with an equitable master contract? On what basis should we define seniority—time in the branch, the bank, the industry? The responsibilities were great. A flaw in the contract might have serious repercussions for years. And there were no outside experts here—we were the experts on bank workers.

To prepare for the first contract conference to be held in September, members in certified branches were requested by the Executive to compile our contract demands and send them to the union office.

Denise Poupard describes what happened in her branch:

In Port McNeill, we had great fun at our meetings, ideas flying so fast that it was difficult to get them all down on paper. This was what the wait had been for—a contract—and our quieter members began to shine. Throughout our involvement with the union, branch management continually attempted to divide us by claiming that certain members had no idea what they were getting into and had been dragged into the union by a few other members. It was typical of management—that they thought workers were not capable of thinking for themselves. While we all chose varying degrees of involvement in the union and had varying views of our potential success, we all saw unionization as the only way of changing our work situation. As we came up with contract ideas, the strong views of all members were vividly apparent. Obviously, everybody had done a lot of thinking about the contract. I was pleasantly surprised to find out that often the best thought out as well as the most radical ideas came from the quietest members.

Some of those initial proposals dealt with conditions peculiar to our branch and other branches in isolated areas but, relying heavily on the SORWUC contract at Electrical Trades Credit Union, we attempted to deal with the basic problems of bank employees.

Looking back, those initial ideas seem somewhat unsophisticated in their wording. We were momentarily too excited to do much more than get down the basic thoughts. But as we attended conventions, read other contracts and generally became more involved in our contract we became increasingly confident in our wording and our ideas—and increasingly demanding.

On September 10 and 11, the first contract conference was held in Vancouver. Approximately fifty members from certified branches and non-certified branches attended. Members from Melfort and Regina, our two certified branches in Saskatchewan, had managed to fly in for the weekend! We sent four representatives from Port McNeill, two of us old pros at union meetings and conventions and two novices who, though very excited, lacked confidence in their ability to function at such a convention. Although only 350 kilometres from Vancouver, our geographical position on northern Vancouver Island necessitated our flying to and from the meeting.

Due to the plane schedule, we were late, arriving in the midst of presentations by Emerald Murphy of AUCE and Angus Macphee of the PPWC. Both speakers offered practical advice.

Angus talked about local and master contracts. The PPWC negotiating committee includes delegates from each plant and all members vote on the union proposals for the master contract before they are presented to the employers. Local issues are dealt with in local negotiations, and each local votes to accept or reject the master contract.

Emerald warned us about mystifying the negotiating process. "We're the best negotiators there are," she said "since we know first hand why certain clauses are needed in the contract." She had been chairperson of AUCE's first negotiating committee. Although some critics view worker negotiators as a bit of a joke. AUCE's inexperienced negotiators had succeeded, only a few years earlier, in bargaining an excellent first contract for 1200 clerical and library workers (95% of whom were women) at the University of British Columbia.

The afternoon of that first day of the first convention was spent on workshops. As there were four workshops, we were able to have one representative from Port McNeill in each of them. Each workshop dealt with one basic area. Workshop One concerned wages and job classifications; Two: vacations and hours of work; Three: working conditions and benefits; Four: seniority, transfers and promotion, job security, union security and union rights.

Considering that SORWUC was not a rich union, most out-of-town representatives were billeted at Vancouver members' homes, but because our novice representatives were shy about staying with people they did not know well, the Port McNeill contingent stayed in a hotel near the convention hall. As this was also where the Saskatchewan representatives stayed, we spent the evening sharing stories and complaints about the banks, union talking and generally having a good time. This was typical of our union sisterhood—complete strangers could get together and feel like old comrades.

The next morning we heard reports from each workshop and then discussed the make-up of our negotiating committee and whether we wanted one contract for everyone or a separate contract for each branch. As we started out the day with CBC television filming, we re-arranged seating so that members who did not wish to be seen on TV, mostly those from non-certified branches, would be safely off-camera.

We decided the contract committee would consist of one representative from each certified branch, one member-at-large representing non-certified branches, and one National Executive officer. While we had only fourteen certified branches at the time, we hoped that this contract would soon become a contract for all bank workers. Therefore, we decided that all members would vote on the contract proposals we would present to the banks, although only members in certified branches would ratify the contract at the conclusion of negotiations. All proposals were to be mailed to each UBW member and voted on by referendum ballot.

The discussion regarding how we were to negotiate—bank, branch or industry-wide—became one of the most important issues at the conference. We decided that it was to the benefit of all bank workers that conditions in the industry be standardized. We could not see why salary, benefits, overtime policy, etc. should be different from branch to branch or bank to bank. We realized, of course, that there would be some specific issues that would have to be negotiated separately, but after an industry-wide contract was negotiated, we could then negotiate individual sub-contracts dealing with concerns specific to each branch.

Cost was also an important factor. The most efficient and cheapest way to negotiate would be with all the banks. An industry-wide contract would represent both present union members and future bank worker members. We wanted to draw up contract proposals that bank workers in B.C. could support. We wanted to use our proposals as an organizing tool. A good first contract would inspire bank workers to join our union.

For me, the most triumphant moment as a union member was the vote on the proposal for the starting wage. Based on only the very basic requirements of a single parent with one child, we finally arrived at a figure of $1,140 per month or $7.50 per hour. While a few members felt this would be an excessive increase (approximately an 80% increase over the banks' base wage of $625-$660 per month in 1977), the majority felt this would be a fair salary that could be justified by cost of living statistics. The average salary in B.C. as determined by the Department of Labour in February, 1977 was $1,185.12 per month. The vote became ecstatic clapping and a celebration of the fact that we were doing the impossible— telling the Canadian chartered banks that we deserved a decent wage.

Workshop One also dealt with re-classifying jobs, but realizing that this was a mammoth task, the issue was carried over to the second conference and eventually left for a committee that would bargain with the banks after our first contract was signed.

Out of Workshop Two came important proposals demanding a thirty-five hour standard work week, twelve paid holidays (including International Women's Day), double time for overtime and voluntary overtime paid on a daily basis.

Workshop Three proposals dealt with breaks, staff rooms, vacations, medical and dental plans, special leave (maternity, paternity, adoption, etc.), the maintenance of replacement staff and adequate training programs for new employees. The issues of seniority and of union security discussed by Workshop Four were tabled until the next conference.

Due to plane and ferry schedules and the demands of distance travelling, many members including those from Port McNeill, were required to leave early. The last decision before people left concerned whether we should release our proposals to the press. There was a brief argument contrasting the importance of secrecy with the value of a sympathetic public acquainted with our demands. Mainly, we saw our contract as an organizing tool and keeping it secret from the banks meant keeping it secret from other bank workers. We publicized the demands, emphasizing that they were mere proposals until voted on by our membership.

The two Port McNeill members for whom the Vancouver conference had been their first United Bank Workers meeting, had been greatly impressed by what they saw and participated in. Discovering that the other representatives were all common ordinary bank workers like themselves, they experienced a boost to their self-confidence and their understanding and appreciation of SORWUC's philosophies.

The Nanaimo contract conference, held two weeks later, presented serious travel problems for the Port McNeill branch. Although geographically closer, we would have to fly to Vancouver, then, as we would miss the plane connection, take the ferry to Nanaimo. But inconvenient plane and ferry schedules were such that it meant missing most of the conference. The only option was an eight hour drive down-island over a gravel road. Due to the travel difficulties and various family commitments, we sent only one representative to the Nanaimo conference.

This conference began with a discussion concerning women's historical role as a source of cheap labour. Once again, we divided into workshops to work on specific areas of the contract. During the two days, there were some serious disagreements. One such area concerned the rights of part-time employees. Some representatives viewed part-time employment as a matter of choice and felt that part-time workers should not be entitled to the same benefits as full-time workers, whether or not these benefits were on a pro rata basis. The majority felt that part-time workers should have the same rights as full-time workers. There are many reasons for working part-time; however many of us saw it as a women's rights issue. Most part-time workers are women who have another full-time job to go home to—raising a family.

Particularly thorny was the issue of defining seniority for part-time employees. Eventually, we worked out an agreeable system based on the number of days worked per week. A conservative minority was out-voted by those who saw protection of part-time worker rights not only as just, but as necessary insurance against our employer replacing full-time workers with less costly part-time workers. To represent these views in negotiations, a part-time employee was elected to the contract committee.

Another source of contention was the access of common-law dependents to medical, dental and optical plans. Finally, we decided that fears of convenient relationships for the sake of dental costs were illogical.

There were also heated discussions concerning what sort of union security clause we wanted, eventually coming down to a choice between union shop (all present and future employees must join the union) and modified union shop (non-members at time of certification do not have to join the union but all future employees must join). Opinion was sufficiently divided to provide for a choice between the two on the referendum ballot.

The issue of seniority was eventually resolved by devising a complicated formula whereby seniority for wages, holidays, promotion, etc., was calculated in different ways—some by time in one branch and others by time in the industry.

During both contract conferences, executive meetings were held. Discussions at these meetings reflected our growing emphasis on organizing the province or region. The Saturday evening executive meeting in Nanaimo was a semi-hysterical affair. Our chances of success, from the beginning, must have been a great deal less than infinitesimal. We were doing what larger, wealthier, more experienced unions considered impossible. The only reason we existed, was that we were the only people crazy enough to try breaking the banks and while we might not succeed, we had already left a crack in their walls that would never go away. We were an impossibility. We were broke, trusting in a lot of hard work, a bit of luck, and a touch of justice to take us as far as we could go. There was little we could do but laugh.

After the two conferences, most of the work was done by the Contract Committee and the office volunteers who did research, typing and innumerable other tasks. Some branches did further work on contract proposals. In Port McNeill we drew on various contracts and our own brains to develop proposals in several areas. Such work then went to the union office for typing and copying, to the Contract Committee for discussion and tighter wording, then to referendum ballot.

All proposals were voted on in referendum. Whenever it appeared opinion was not clear on any proposal, further information or arguments for and against were mailed out with the referendum. Union security, definition of seniority and International Women's Day were a few of the proposals which received such clarification.

In Port McNeill, we frequently had meetings and discussions to solve any confusion about the meaning and implications of the proposals before we voted. Basically our branch members agreed on everything. There was some initial uncertainty as to whether we preferred a union shop or a modified union shop. It was difficult to keep personal feelings out of some decisions such as union security. In working out our proposed pay scale, we had to try to separate our respect for certain employees from the classification level of their respective jobs.

One fortunate result of the first conference was that one woman now had sufficient confidence to become our main Contract Committee representative. After each meeting, she would discuss the meeting with other branch members so we would be kept up to date. As notice was given to begin bargaining November 1, contract committee meetings in Vancouver were very frequent.

By the time we started bargaining with the banks, we were well acquainted with our contract proposals. The work at conferences on proposals and on referendums was an educational process on how to write our own contract. UBW members had had great help from other SORWUC members, especially people working in the Vancouver office. We had also received advice and help from other unions. We could be proud of a contract that we had written ourselves. But now, effectively, the question of success was out of our hands. The word was out that we were trying to unionize the banks. We had broken the sod and gotten far enough to have drawn up our contract and given notice to bargain. The rest was up to the majority of bank workers who had been silently waiting to see what would happen to us. The crucial point had arrived. If they joined, we could go all the way. Without them, there was not going to be a contract signed.

Well my girl she runs the office, you know that's what girls do
She does her job, yes very well, and most of my job too
But it's certainly outrageous, it's completely out of line
When she demands a salary commensurate with mine.
— "The Bosses' Lament" by T. Dash

11   Meet You at the 'Y'

SORWUC National Union, 1114-207 W. Hastings, Vancouver, B.C.
Sept. 26, 1977

Mr. G.T. Robertson,   Mr. E.S. Duffield
Sr. Vice-President, Personnel,   Sr. Vice-President, Human Resources,
Head Office, Bank of Montreal   Canadian Imperial Bank of Commerce
129 St. James St. W.,   Head Office, Commerce Court West,
Montreal, Quebec   Toronto, Ont.

Mr. F.M. Goddard,
General Manager, Personnel,
Bank of Nova Scotia
44 King St. W.
Toronto, Ont.

Dear Sirs,
    In accordance with Sections 146 and 148 of the Canada Labour
Code, Part V, we hereby give notice that we wish to commence bargaining for the purpose of entering into a collective agreement.
    Our proposal is that our first meeting for the purpose of bargain-
ing be on November 1, 1977 at 10:00 a.m. at the Y.W.C.A. Building,
580 Burrard St., Vancouver, B.C. We have taken the liberty of booking
Room 201.
    We look forward to hearing from you in the near future.

Yours sincerely,
Jean Rands, National President

Copies to Canada Labour Relations Board; Managers of all certified
branches; R.J. Kavanagh, General Manager, B.C. Region, Bank of Nova
Scotia; G.T. Orrston, Regional General Manager, B.C. & Yukon Region,
CIBC; M.E. Nesmith, Sr. Vice-President, B.C. Region, Bank of Montreal

This letter was sent to the banks. Their responses ranged from
'confused' to 'outraged' that we would suggest they meet with their
competition in industry-wide negotiations. We received letters from
them stating they were not clear as to our intentions and that the
CLRB granted certification to individual branches and that they were
going to negotiate on a branch basis.
    Members in certified branches by now had elected their rep to the
Contract Committee. The committee met regularly to finalize our proposals and generally prepare for negotiations. At one meeting the
committee decided that in order to get to the bargaining table we would
agree to meet with each bank separately with the intention of again
proposing industry wide negotiations.

By mid-December initial meetings had been held with the Scotia, the Bank of Montreal and the Commerce. The discussions and arguments in these initial meetings were the same with all three banks. We discussed procedural problems such as how often we were going to meet, where we were going to meet, whether we would meet during the day or in the evenings, and so on. We proposed that negotiations take place during the day. We made it clear that the union would pay the employees' wages for the days spent in negotiations. We argued that negotiating a first contract takes a long time and it is important that both parties be alert and well rested for each session. Bank workers shouldn't be expected to work all day and then negotiate in the evenings. We also pointed out that responsibilities at home for bank workers who were mothers meant that they couldn't possibly attend evening sessions on a regular basis. The Scotia and the Commerce refused to meet during the day.

Our committee proposed that we meet on a regular basis, perhaps two or three days a week at the YWCA in Vancouver. The banks wanted to meet in hotel rooms. The extra expense was not an obstacle to them. The Commerce proposed that since they intended to negotiate on a branch basis, we should meet "on location", meaning for example, that we would fly to Port McNeill to meet in a hotel room to negotiate for the Port McNeill branch.

We discussed our determination to negotiate an industry wide contract. We argued that as our negotiating committee consisted of one rep from each certified branch, the same committee was going to negotiate each contract. It would be time consuming to meet separately regarding each branch. We assumed that the banks would have the same questions and arguments for each of our proposals so it seemed a waste of time to repeat them. We also didn't want twenty-one contracts expiring at different times throughout the year as that would mean both parties would be in negotiations all year long.

The banks argued that "collective bargaining should follow the basis on which the union sought and achieved certification—the individual branch unit." The Scotia argued that the contracts would not be the same nor would they even be similar, and that each branch was unique and must have a contract dealing with its own particular problems and working conditions. Each bank was horror-struck that we would expect them to meet with their "opposition". After our first negotiating meeting with the Scotia, they sent us a ten page submission in response to our proposal for "multi-bank" collective bargaining. They stated, among other things, that banks are "not a government sanctioned monopoly but a competitive profit-motivated enterprise". That was to explain why they could not negotiate important matters together with their "competitors". They claimed that industry-wide bargaining wouldn't work because each bank had a different emphasis on the type of customer it tended to attract! They also claimed that arranging meetings with all the banks' bargaining teams would create an atmosphere conducive to far greater delays than meeting with one bank. In response to our argument that other industries negotiated on an industry wide basis the Scotia replied that this practice was "developed". Negotiating a collective agreement in banks was a new experience for all of us, they said, and we should "develop" our own method of negotiating over the years. . . Last but not least, they said that as the CLRB had ruled the branch to be an appropriate bargaining unit, we should negotiate that way.

The Bank of Montreal stated: "It is important for all branch managers to be present at the sessions. The success in administering a collective agreement will in large part be particularly dependent on the understanding and appreciation of the branch management. To have a meeting with the managers from all certified branches present would be unwieldy."

These arguments about the crucial role of the manager differed drastically from those put forward at the hearings when the banks claimed that the only appropriate bargaining unit was the Nation. Then they swore that managers only carry out policy and decisions made in Head Office, have no authority to settle grievances and that working conditions are basically the same in each branch.

It became clear that the banks would not budge from their position. Finally the Contract Committee agreed that we would negotiate with each bank separately and we proposed to negotiate a master agree-

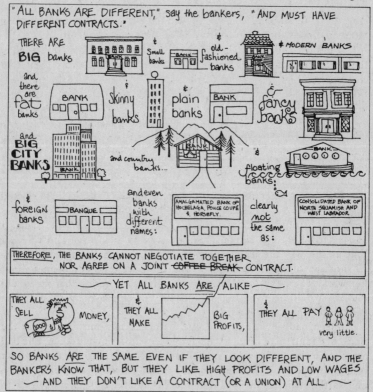

ment for all certified branches within each bank. In response to this the banks repeated many of the same arguments. They once again threw the bargaining unit decision at us, the difficulty for all branch managers to be present at all sessions, and so forth. Although we had the best arguments for our proposal in terms of efficiency, expediency and arriving at what would, in effect, be a master contract for each bank, the banks were not impressed. They ignored all our arguments and insisted we negotiate on a branch basis.

What could we do? We did not have the bargaining power to insist on negotiating our way. We set up meetings with the banks to begin negotiations for various branches although our contract proposals were the same for each branch of each bank and we realized that when a contract was negotiated for one branch it would certainly set a precedent for the other branches. The Commerce insisted on its original proposal of meeting "on location" and refused to give time off for contract committee reps to negotiate during the day. This proposal had grave implications for our Committee. It would be virtually impossible for the Commerce reps to attend a meeting on Vancouver Island after working all day in a branch and then return home in time for work the next day. It also meant greater expenses for us.

Members of the Committee were still meeting regularly on weekends and in the evenings. We were becoming more familiar with our contract proposals, getting to know each other better and becoming more confident about our ability to negotiate our own contract.

Although the banks were ready to sit down at the bargaining table, they were by no means prepared to accept unionization. They told employees in non-union branches that their wages would be frozen if they joined the union and they continued to harass and intimidate union members in certified branches. Sometimes the Contract Committee representative was treated like a shop steward—changes in the branch were announced to the union rep first and the rep would relay messages to management on behalf of the other employees. In some branches, the union rep was singled out for attack. This was the case at the Bank of Commerce on the Sechelt peninsula.

The union members at the Commerce in Gibsons had elected Eileen Quigley to represent them on the union Contract Committee, with Carol Dulyk as her alternate. On September 28, the manager had visited Eileen at home while she was on sick leave and told her that as she was the least senior employee she was being laid off due to shortage of work. He stressed that there were no complaints about her work. The next day she was given a letter promising that she would that she would be given first opportunity of employment should it be necessary to hire at the branch.

Eileen had signed up the Royal branches and our members at the Bank of Montreal, as well as the employees at her own branch. She had attended union meetings in Vancouver and Nanaimo to discuss contract proposals, spoken to the press on the Peninsula, and was seen by everyone as the main union organizer there. Lay-offs are extremely rare in banks and bank workers on the Peninsula were shocked, particularly as Eileen had given up a full-time permanent position at another bank in order to start work at the Commerce just four months earlier. Carol and others told the manager at a staff meeting that they thought Eileen had been laid off for union activity. Eileen continued to be active in the union although Carol Dulyk replaced her as official representative of the branch on the Contract Committee.

Sometime in December 1977, Carol talked at a Contract Committee meeting about she was afraid of losing her job because of her union activity. She also did a TV interview on the subject.

On Saturday, January 21, 1978, the manager asked Carol to stay behind for a few minutes after work. Carol describes what happened:

"He proceded to show me the unit count from Regional Office and informed me that our count was way below standard. One staff member would have to be laid off, and that person was me. He said I had the opportunity of transferring to a branch in Vancouver and that I could commute daily. I said that was a very impractical move for me because of ferry scheduling and that I had also informed him of my husband's upcoming open heart surgery on January 31, which was why I requested holidays starting February 2. I stated that I had more seniority, if only by a month, than the teller he was keeping on, and that she would be quitting by March of this year. He said he knew all that but it was his decision, based on the fact that she could put through more items in a day than I could. I told him that was a pile of garbage, and that all one had to do was look through the tellers books to prove that false. I told him that I figured something like this was in the wind, since the last altercation I had with him, and that I felt he was discriminating against me because of my union activities. He suggested that I see what the union could do for me. I said that if nothing else I would picket the branch myself. He said they would give me one month's pay and a letter stating that I would be the first one called back if there was an opening. He then asked me for my keys and I said I would release them on receipt of the letter or separation slip. He also showed me a letter from Regional Office in reply to a letter of his sent on December 17, 1977. It was an acknowledgement of his request for a reduction of staff by one. I mentioned to him that I had done a TV interview in which I had said that I felt my job was in jeopardy because of my union activity."

Carol came to the union office on the following Monday, January 23.

A union rep called the regional personnel manager of the Commerce and told him that as Carol was the senior teller we could only assume she was terminated because of her union activity. He claimed that Carol was the last hired and they they had been reasonable in offering her a transfer to Vancouver or one month's pay in lieu of notice. He agreed that the bank normally laid people off in order of seniority. He also agreed that layoffs were unusual. The rep insisted that Carol was the most senior teller and urged him to reconsider the decision. She told him we would lay a complaint of unfair labour practice.

We drafted this complaint and got it to the Canada Labour Relations Board that same day. But this was such a serious attack on our union we couldn't leave it to a long, slow legal process. We had to confront the bank publicly. Many bank workers were afraid of losing their jobs. We had to prove that the union was prepared to defend our members. We drafted petitions and press releases, and made plans for a public campaign to protest the bank's action.

The following day there were two more conversation with the same regional manager. This time he said the decision was made on the basis of performance rather than seniority. The most recent performance report had been done September 17 of the previous year and Carol was rated as responsible and competent. The manager had added the following comment to the report: "Mrs. Dulyk is doing a good job in her position as teller. She gets along well with customers and staff." That was before she represented the union.

Carol was determined to fight the case. On February 1, her first day "laid off", she began standing in front of the bank during business hours asking customers to sign a petition asking the bank to reinstate her. Eileen Quigley joined Carol in petitioning and picketing in front of the bank. Other trade unionists from Gibsons joined in the picket as did SORWUC members and supporters from Vancouver.

On February 3, Carol and Jean went into the bank to see the manager and told him that the union was prepared to put up a fight to get Carol's job back, that we didn't want to damage the business of the branch but that the longer the fight went on, the more likely it was to damage the branch. We said we were anxious to settle the problem, and he indicated he would also like to do that. However, he later called the union office and said the bank was not prepared to change their decision although they were prepared to offer both Carol and Eileen some relief work.

Carol told the manager that she wouldn't picket until after the bank's representatives had met with an officer of the Board to discuss possible settlement of the dispute. She continued to ask customers to sign the petition. The meetings between the Board's officer and the bank's representatives were not successful so picketing was resumed.

Carol worked hard to build community support for her case, and for the union. She spoke at local union meetings and at meetings of community groups and senior citizens. The Sechelt Teachers Association issues a press release protesting the lay-off. The Canadian Paperworkers Union (CPU), the Ferry Workers, the Fishermens' Union and the IWA had all identified themselves with the protest campaign.

In three weeks, 500 Gibsons' residents signed the petition asking the bank to reinstate Carol. This petition was presented to the Commerce Regional Office on February 21 and the matter was continually raised at negotiations along with other unfair labour practice complaints.

Now the bosses get together
And they act real smart
They do everything they can
To keep us workers apart
— "We Gotta Have Union" based on
a traditional gospel song

12   A Change of Plans

The UBW decided to hold a special convention on January 29, 1978 to reassess our organizing strategy.

The following motion, proposed jointly by the UBW Executive and Contract Committee, was to be discussed at this convention: "That we stop applying for branches and apply to the Canada Labour Relations Board for the province as the bargaining unit as soon as possible."

Linda Read, a UBW Executive member who had quit her job at Mastercharge a few months earlier, worked on a volunteer basis in the union office. She describes the special convention:

Forty bank workers, including a member from Saskatchewan, attended the convention in Vancouver. There was a great deal of enthusiasm amongst us. Only seventeen months earlier the first meeting of bank workers in SORWUC had been held. Now, we were going to discuss the launching of a provincial drive. Before we began our discussion on organizing strategy, we heard reports on the present state of the UBW.

I reported on the banks' recently announced wage freeze in certified branches. As early as July, 1977, individual managers all over the province were saying that wages would be frozen if employees joined the union. By fall, branches were rife with rumours. We attempted to dispel the rumours with a leaflet describing Section 148 of the Canada Labour Code. This section states that the employer cannot change conditions of employment during the course of negotiations unless the union consents to such changes. We understood that this section of the Code would prevent an employer from either bribing employees to not join the union or punishing those employees who did join. As the annual cost of living increases were a condition of employment, our position was that withholding these increases would be grounds for an unfair labour practice complaint.

On December 14, we sent a "Letter of Understanding" to all the banks. We asked them to agree to sign this letter which stated: "While negotiations are in progress, any general improvements in wages, benefits, or working conditions, which are implemented generally in branches throughout B.C., shall also be implemented in those branches for which the union holds certification . . ."

The banks' responses to our "Letter of Understanding" were identical. If we were prepared to ratify a first contract with a five percent wage increase, they would be prepared to sign our letter.

We refused to agree to such a contract. We deserved more. In addition, such an agreement would have had a serious effect on organizing. If we were to agree to a five percent wage increase before negotiations began, there would be no material incentive to join the union. Also, we thought it would be disastrous to lock certified branches into a five percent increase. When the AIB wage controls were lifted, non-union branches could get a higher increase.

In January 1978 we filed unfair labour practice complaints against the Royal Bank and the Bank of Nova Scotia for withholding the wage increases.

After my report we had a lengthy debate on the proposed motion. What the motion meant was that we would continue to sign up individual bank workers all over the province and when we had a majority (or thirty-five percent for a vote) signed up in a particular bank, we would apply for certification for the whole province as the bargaining unit.

At this time, few bank workers were joining the union. Organizing a provincial unit meant that bank workers could join the union without forfeiting their annual wage increase. It also meant that bank workers could join the union anonymously. When small branches applied for certification there was no way union membership could be kept a secret.

Another argument for the proposed motion was that members in non-certified branches could play a more active role in the union. They could work within an autonomous committee in their community to organize their area.

The main argument for the province as the bargaining unit, however,

---

UBW Branches in B.C.

24 branches certified on the following dates

Commerce Port McNeill July 19, 1977
B of M Langley July 19, 1977
B of M Port Alberni July 19, 1977
B of M Ganges July 19, 1977
B of M Edmonds & Kingsway July 19, 1977
Commerce Gibsons August 16, 1977
Commerce Brookswood August 16, 1977
B of M Georgia & Seymour August 25, 1977
B of M West Vancouver Main Branch August 31, 1977
Commerce Ganges September 6, 1977
Scotia SFU September 6, 1977
Scotia Vancouver Heights September 6, 1977
B of M Powell River September 12, 1977
B of M Royal Oak (Victoria) September 22, 1977
B of M Newton October 6, 1977
B of M North Van October 26, 1977
Scotia Edmonds & 6th October 28, 1977
Royal Gibsons November 3, 1977
B of M Fortune Centre (Kamloops) November 4, 1977
Royal Sahali (Kamloops) November 4, 1977
Commerce Mission November 21, 1977
Montreal Westview January 20, 1978
TD Tahsis February 9, 1978
Commerce Creston June 30, 1978

was the incredible bargaining power such a unit would have.

Some members questioned whether or not we had the finances and resources to sign up the whole province. Some people also said that if a branch had a majority and wanted to be certified, it was their right.

We finally voted that we would not apply for any more branches and would go for the province. Only one person voted against the motion.

Data Centres, Chargex and Mastercharge Centres were in a different situation in that they were larger than branches. The problem for workers wasn't anonymity; it was communication. They had more bargaining power and different working conditions. Organizers from one data centre reported that they had signed up about twenty-five percent of the employees and hoped to be able to apply soon. The convention authorized the Executive, together with organizers in the particular bank, to decide whether or not to apply for certification for large centres as separate units.

We then discussed how we were going to sign up the province. Our attention focussed on organizing committees. We had been discussing organizing committees in a somewhat abstract way for a few months. At the convention it became clear that these committees would be the vehicles for organizing the province.

Up to that time, organizing efforts were totally dependent on the Vancouver office. Heather, myself and other UBW Executive members would meet interested bank workers on lunch hours, or before and after work. If they didn't live close to Vancouver, packages of information would be sent to them and eventually a meeting would be arranged.

The provincial drive could not be organized from Vancouver. Downtown Vancouver was very weak in terms of membership. There were now bank workers all over the province who knew enough about the UBW to answer any questions arising out of a first organizing meeting. These workers needed to set up autonomous organizations to make decisions regarding their own drives. We saw each organizing committee as an embryo of a union local. They would make decisions about fundraising and publicity and would rally support from women's groups and other unions. They would coordinate leafletting and meet with interested bank workers in their community. Local unions were prepared to give more financial and volunteer assistance to bank workers in their own area in Vancouver. In August 1977 the UBW, by referendum ballot, had voted to turn Local 2 into the UBW Section of SORWUC, with the intention of forming organizing committees within the section. With the UBW membership spread all across B.C., it had become impossible for many members to attend local union meetings and participate in decision making. SORWUC's structure had been changed to allow for the establishment of occupational/industrial sections which would be responsible for industry-wide organizing campaigns and could be authorized to negotiate on behalf of their members.

The Section and the organizing committees would not only be the most effective, but the most democratic structure for the province-wide campaign.

The union office continued to coordinate negotiations for the twenty-two certified branches. We were regularly speaking to the press and to trade unions, and we were always involved in legal hassles of one kind or another. In addition, people in the office were helping to establish the organizing committees, printing a monthly newsletter and researching legal matters. The necessary clerical work was overwhelming for one person. Heather's term had ended. The special convention had voted to amend our UBW Section by-laws to include two union organizer positions on the Executive. These positions were to be full-time, paid at $800 per month, for one year each. The organizers were to be elected by the UBW membership. Three bank workers ran for the two positions. Their statements and a ballot were mailed to all UBW members. Dodie Zerr, a teller from the Commerce, Victory Square, and Sheree Butt, a control clerk from the Bank of Montreal, West Vancouver, were elected and began working at the union office March 1, 1978.

The UBW Section Executive played a major role in assisting members with the beginning phases of their organizing committees. A package containing necessary steps and documents was prepared. It included:
— a condensed version of "rules of order" to assist members in ensuring the meetings ran efficiently and democratically,
— a sample of a letter to the UBW Section Executive requesting a charter for the organizing committee,
— a sample of how to take minutes,
— an example of how to write a press release,
— an example of by-laws which would ensure that the committee be autonomous, democratic and not contradict the UBW Section by-laws.

The organizing committees were composed of members from both certified and non-certified branches. A few inactive members from branches where no majority had been obtained or where the vote was lost, became involved in the union again. By the time we were in a position to have a founding meeting of a committee, the people involved basically knew how it was going to function.

Usually a UBW Executive member from Vancouver attended the founding meeting to give assistance. This meant travelling to somewhere in B.C. and staying with a bank worker for a few days. Often we stayed in the community to help arrange meetings with other trade unionists to tell them what bank workers in their town were doing. We also arranged interviews with the local newspaper, radio and T.V. stations. Sometimes bank workers did the press themselves, but because most of them were still having to deal with pressure from management, it was often better that someone from Vancouver spoke to the press.

These times were hectic. Organizing committees were being set up in various locations around the province including Kamloops, Sechelt, Mission, Powell River and all over Vancouver Island.

The bank workers in the Mission organizing committee requested their charter in March 1978, and after a few meetings had passed their by-laws, elected their executive, opened a bank account and decided how they would organize other bank employees in their jurisdiction. Committee members wrote their own leaflets which addressed bank workers in their towns. They organized volunteers to help leaflet local bank branches. Still, bank workers did not join.

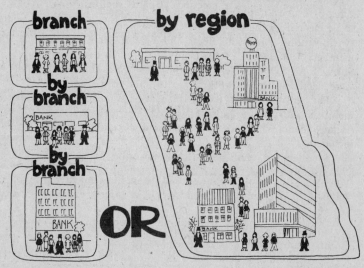

No organizing committee could sign up a majority of bank workers in their jurisdiction. The wage freeze and the banks' intimidation had done the job.

As well, union members were having trouble on the home front. An important factor to our success (and sanity) was moral support at home and in our communities. After all, on how many fronts could we wage battles? Unfortunately, not all of us had this support. Some members took on more responsibility than others. There was some resentment of those who did not participate. One bank worker aired her anger in a letter to the union office in which she analyzed the situation in her branch. She said that a few women "suffered" from husbands or boyfriends who:

"a) did not trust their wives away from them in the big city.
b) preferred their wives to earn low wages as it encouraged financial dependency (and, in their minds, marital stability)
c) could not manage to feed and take care of themselves if wives were away for a meeting."

There were, of course, women who could not attend meetings because they were single mothers and could not afford to pay baby-sitters. One woman found a way to attend most meetings although she was a single mother with three children and had two part-time jobs besides her job at the bank. There were also women who were so determined to work in SORWUC that they ended up taking on the banks and non-supportive husbands at the same time.

Generally, when we spoke to women's groups, the NDP and other unions, the people we addressed were supportive. Even groups or unions that were not in a financial position to donate money to SORWUC offered volunteers, the use of office machines and space in the offices to hold our meetings. Unions such as PPWC, AUCE and others not only gave us moral support but they contributed financial help as well. Women's groups contributed many volunteer leafletters as well as providing moral support.

But sometimes we had to deal with less rewarding confrontations. On occasion, we were met with accusations from the CLC affiliated unions about how "independent unions were dividing the trade union movement" and "SORWUC doesn't have the resources or expertise to service its members or continue the drive". As one UBW member reported after meeting with a union business agent: "I felt as though I was at a job interview." When I walked into a Nanaimo union office, the first words the business agent said to me were "We hate independent unions. We think all unions should be in the mainstream of labour—the CLC." After our discussion though, he offered us the use of a type-writer and office space.

The B.C. Government Employees Union (BCGEU) had been very enthusiastic about our campaign in the summer of 1977. They gave us a $1000 donation and their administrative support component gave us a $5000 interest-free loan. We used their meeting rooms free of charge. However, after August 1977 we received no further financial support from them. And in the fall Laraine Singler, an assistant general secretary of the BCGEU who had tried for months to convince UBW executive members that we should split from SORWUC to join the CLC, was appointed to direct the CLC's bank campaign from Ottawa.

Many members of CLC affiliated unions had wives, daughters and mothers working in banks and SORWUC had been the most successful thus far in organizing banks. Why were unions who had supported us in the past now withdrawing support? Had the CLC Executive ordered affiliates not to support us any more? The CLC had begun their own organizing campaign, directed from Ottawa. (There were also other CLC affiliates that held certifications in the banks—OTEU, RCIU, Steelworkers).

In December of 1977 we became aware of a letter from the CLC executive to all local unions and labour councils in B.C. This letter announced the launching of the CLC national campaign to organize bank workers. Laraine Singler, assistant general secretary of the BCGEU, was moving to Ottawa and would coordinate the campaign. The letter said that all unions were to support this campaign and no other campaign.

This certainly contradicted what Donald Montgomery, then secretary-treasurer of the CLC, stated in a letter to us July 19, 1977, " . . . it is imperative that organizing drives afford the workers the opportunity to become members of the union of their choice." The CLC directive ignored the well known fact that SORWUC was negotiating with the banks and launching a provincial drive. Several unions and one labour council wrote letters to the CLC protesting this directive.

Our National Executive had been corresponding with the CLC Executive since July 1977. In October we sent a letter to the CLC saying that our National Executive would be prepared to recommend to our members that SORWUC affiliate to the CLC if they were prepared to accept us as a National Union, without changing our structure or objectives. On December seventh we sent an urgent request for funds when we learned that the Royal Bank intended to appeal the branch-by-branch decision to the Federal Court of Appeals. That decision was crucial for all unions involved in bank organizing and we wanted help to defend it. In December Joe Morris, then CLC president, wrote to the UBW Section Executive. He said that the CLC was prepared to accept the UBW Section into the CLC and that once the UBW had joined the CLC's national effort, they would then consider paying our outstanding bills. As far as the rest of SORWUC was concerned, the CLC said they would look at each of our individual units and see how they overlapped with the jurisdiction of the CLC affiliated unions. Our understanding of this proposal was that SORWUC as a union would no longer exist, and the certifications that we held in Local 1 would be transferred to the "appropriate" CLC union that claimed jurisdiction of that particular industry. Bank workers did not want to split from SORWUC.

The UBW Section Executive unanimously rejected their proposal. We wrote the CLC and stated that we saw no use in further correspondence. The special convention in January endorsed the Executive's decision.

It was a bitter lesson for us to find that solidarity did not include us. After all the platitudes spoken about organizing the unorganized, the CLC showed no signs of support or encouragement when someone actually set out to do it.

Whoever do they think they are to organize like men?
Well I believe in order, the tried and trusted norm
I'll damn well see her fired, if I can find the form.
—"The Bosses' Lament" by T. Dash

13   Legal Knots

Our attempts to get the banks to negotiate the issue of the wage freeze failed. We filed unfair labour practice complaints against the Scotia and the Royal in January 1978 alleging that:

1. denying salary and other improvements to certified branches was discrimination against the certified branches.
2. withholding improvements had the effect of intimidating employees at non-union branches and discouraging them from joining the union.
3. the banks' actions interfered with the union's representation of employees at the certified branches.

The Board announced a hearing to begin February 20. We had always felt more in control when doing our own representation at LRB Hearings so we decided not to have a lawyer represent us. We believed that we would be better able than a lawyer to explain the effect the wage freeze had on our organizing. So we decided that Jean should represent the union with help from Charlotte and Jackie and everyone else who was available. Although we understood that legally and technically our case was not strong, we felt strongly that we were right. The wage freeze was an anti-union act violating our right to organize and the future of our whole campaign could depend on this case.

The complaint against the Royal was heard first. The witnesses from the bank's Regional Office in Vancouver admitted that they had gone to speak to employees at the certified branches to explain that the wage increase they were giving to non-union branches was the very best possible under the Anti-Inflation Board. They said the reason their branch wouldn't get the increase was because the union had refused to accept it as the wage package for our first union contract. We argued that bank management had violated the Labour Code by attempting to negotiate with individual employees, rather than with all of us collectively through the union. A union member from the Kamloops branch testified that the response of employees there was to look for a way to get out of the union so that they could get the wage increase. Jackie testified that the wage freeze was discouraging employees from joining the union. Our evidence on this last point was not strong. It's obvious that if people make more money in non-union branches, that will discourage them from joining the Union. But how do you prove why people aren't joining the union? If they won't join, they're not likely to agree to testify on behalf of the union about why they won't.

It's clear that if the bank had withheld wage increases from union members only, that would be illegal discrimination. However, the bank was punishing all employees in certified branches, even those who had always adamantly opposed the union. Jean tried hard to convince the Board that discriminating against two branches out of 200 in B.C. had the same effect on the union drive as discriminating against individual union members.

The Royal hearing only took one day.

The next morning we started on the Scotia complaints. The bank had come up with a dozen reasons why the Board should not even hear these complaints. They were submitted either one or two days after the time limit in the Code. (We miscounted the days!) They were submitted on behalf of all employees in the certified branches although not all the employees had signed them. The bank claimed the union had not given enough facts (as if the bank didn't know the facts). And no one in the certified branches had the right amount of seniority to benefit from the bank's new vacation policy, so they hadn't lost anything by being denied this improvement.

An entire day was spent in complicated legal arguments on these questions. Frantically flipping through the Code, Jean and Charlotte did a good job of answering the bank's lawyer. We couldn't let the Board throw the whole campaign out on technicalities. We lost some of these arguments, but won enough that the Board decided to hear evidence on the main issue—the wage freeze.

The next morning Jean had the flu. She asked for an adjournment of a few days. The Board agreed to adjourn until the next day! We went back to the union office in a panic.

Pat Barter, who walked into the union office at 11:00 a.m. that day, tells what happened next:

I was working evening shift as a waitress and spending my afternoons at the union office. As National second vice-president, my responsibility was the National newsletter; I was also assisting a bargaining unit of homemakers in Powell River who were in the midst of their first negotiations.

Linda zeroed in on me as soon as I walked in the door. "What are you doing tomorrow, Pat?" "Depends," I said. (You learned to approach these questions warily in the union office, particularly when the asker looked agitated.) "You have to do the hearings on the wage freeze. Jean's sick. You've done hearings for Local 1 in front of the B.C. Board and everyone else is either working or negotiating. We'll help you."

What could I do? After all, when I had joined with my co-workers to get our first contract somebody said to me—'we can do it ourselves'— and we did, but with help from others. I guess my turn had come.

There was much shuffling of date books as people shifted schedules so they could cover one another and help me. Jackie (who was on sick leave recovering from surgery— and Charlotte said they would sit at the hearing table with me. We went into a group brainstorming session that covered the law, the facts, our case, the bank's rebuttal, how to lay out our questions and what to wear when going before the Board. I walked off to work in a daze.

When I got off at midnight Jackie was waiting for me at home and together we went over all the questions we would put to our witnesses and tried to guess the answers we would get from the bank's witnesses. After a few hours sleep and a big breakfast, we met with the bank workers who were going to testify. More coffee and toast and yogurt and a discussion of strategy and tactics.

First the Board heard the testimony of several bank workers. I asked the questions we hoped would show the Board the depth of the effect of the wage freeze on union members. The bank's lawyer then cross-examined them, trying to show that they had not been individually discriminated against, that they had not been intimidated, that they had not been personally affected by the change in service requirements for vacation, and that they had not been promised a specific wage increase that year.

The personnel director took the stand. He answered briefly and had to be asked several times to expand his answers. We had to prove that the bank was deliberately discouraging unionization by sending a memo to non-certified branches saying that the wage increase would not apply to union branches. But who will admit in front of the Board that they have broken the law? Our last question to him was: "Why did the bank send this memo to non-union branches and not to union branches?" We asked him three times, and each time he seemed to become more curt and actually started to lose his temper. He never really answered that question, particularly when pressed as to why the memo was sent out before the matter had even been raised with the union. He finally said he had thought it would confuse people if it was sent to union branches, and besides the matter was one for the bargaining table at those branches. The bank's lawyers tried to argue that the union was responsible for the delay in negotiations. The Board members then asked a few questions.

The final stage was the presentation of argument. Each side reviewed the evidence, the law, cited other decisions made about the same section of the law and argued why the Board should find in their favour.

The Board's decision was received March 10. They had voted two to one against us. The Board stated that there was no doubt that employees in certified branches were treated differently than employees in non-union branches and that perhaps this had had a "disheartening effect" on some individuals in certified branches and an inhibiting effect on employees in non-union branches. Nonetheless, they agreed with the banks that giving wage increases to workers in certified branches would undercut negotiations and ruled that we hadn't proved the intention of the wage freeze was to smash the union. The Board declared that the employees in union branches chose to opt "out of the realm of unilateral employer action and into the collective bargaining regime".

The third member of the Board disagreed with the decision of the other two and wrote his own opinion. "It is obvious that discrimination of the type practiced here will have and did have the effect of undermining the union."

The banks had won—they could continue the wage freeze with the blessing of the Board. But they weren't satisfied. The Scotia appealed to the Federal Court asking the Court to rule that the Board should have refused to consider our complaints because they were late.

At the time we underestimated the effect of the five percent wage loss on the organizing drive. Members in most of our certified branches responded by getting angry and more determined to negotiate a good contract. It took a long time for us to realize the effect on non-certified branches. The wage loss was both a warning to unorganized branches and a punishment to organized branches. Many bank workers were convinced by the banks to "wait and see" what the union could win for them before they joined and risked losing other benefits. The more waiting and seeing there was, the weaker was the union's bargaining power.

Another blatantly pro-management decision was still to come—that on the Carol Dulyk case.

The hearing on Carol Dulyk's case, which had been set for February 24 was adjourned to March 13 due to the illness of one of the bank's witnesses. Jean, Charlotte, Carol, Eileen and one other member from the Gibsons branch attended, with Jean speaking for the union.

The Commerce's position was that they had to reduce staff because business was slow, and that Carol was the one laid off because her work had suddenly deteriorated. This deterioration just happened to coincide with her becoming union representative for the branch! We felt we had a strong case.

The bank's argument that Carol was less competent than the other teller was contradicted by the bank's own evaluations of her performance which had rated her competent and capable of promotion to assistant accountant. Carol's co-workers testified in her favour. However, the testimony of the manager and accountant was given more weight by the Board than was the testimony of another teller and ledgerkeeper.

It is a basic assumption in this society that management can and does assess employees' work fairly and accurately. It is also a basic assumption that management can and does assess the needs of the business (number of staff, number of branches, etc.) fairly and accurately. In a small branch, this basic assumption about management can put the union and the bank workers at a severe disadvantage. The only people in the branch who can state whether or not someone is competent and have their opinion taken seriously are management.

The Labour Code says that where an employee claims she was fired for union activity, the employer must prove that they did not fire her for union activity. However, in practice, the employer is given the benefit of any doubt. There is no law against firing people. The employer is free to fire people for any reason whatsoever, good or bad, except union activity (or discrimination prohibited by human rights legislation). The union must therefore prove that the **intent** of the firing was to weaken the union. The only way to prove anti-union motivation directly is to get management to admit that they fired the employee for union activity. We weren't too optimistic about getting them to do that, although we tried on cross-examination of the bank's witnesses.

Mostly, we had to rely on circumstantial evidence. We set out to prove:

1. That the effect of the employer's action in firing Carol was anti-union since it removed the union representative from the branch, and weakened the union's majority.
2. That the employer was aware of, and hostile to, Carol's union activity.
3. That the reasons given by the employer for terminating Carol were not the true reasons. We had to undercut their argument that the layoff was an economic necessity. Failing that, we had to argue that Carol, as the senior teller, should not have been the one laid off and that the complaints about Carol's work coincided with her active involvement in the union.
4. That there was a pattern of anti-union activity by management in the branch, including the anti-union meetings and the layoff of Eileen Quigley, the previous rep.

We felt we had strong evidence of anti-union motivation in Carol's dismissal. We brought out the story of the early meetings in the branch following the application for certification, the manager's tears, the employees' response. Eileen told the story of her lay-off, and Carol testified that the employees had seen it as punishment for Eileen's union activity. We demonstrated that the complaints about Carol's work began after she assumed a position of responsibility in the union.

The only way we could deal with the economic argument was to cross-examine the bank's witnesses. Some big shot from Regional Office showed up with piles of charts and statistics purporting to prove that the Gibsons branch was overstaffed compared to other similar branches. We did what we could to use their own, presumably hand-picked statistics, to prove that the Gibsons branch was no more overstaffed than lots of other branches. We asked how many lay-offs there had been in the B.C.-Yukon region in the previous year. Out of 4,500 employees in the Region only ten were laid off that year. Two of those ten were in the Gibsons branch (out of five employees!) The bank agreed that their normal procedure was to reduce staff by waiting for people to quit and then not replacing them.

We also questioned bank management witnesses about the factors involved in deciding whether to increase or decrease the size of a branch. At the hearings about the bargaining unit, the same bank had argued strongly that profitability is not determined on a branch level; that there are many reasons other than economic ones which could determine whether or not a branch is kept open, or how long a new branch is expected to lose money before it becomes established. Clearly, the expansion or reduction of staff in a branch, and even the question of whether a branch is closed, is determined in relation to the bank's policy objectives in the region. The bank did not prove that it had to reduce staff at the Gibsons branch for economic reasons. They admitted they had all kinds of discretion in the matter. However, we were unable to prove that one of their overall policies was to limit the growth of unionism in the branches. This seemed to be obvious but impossible to prove.

It was amazingly difficult to get the bank to admit that Carol had more seniority than the other teller, even though all their own documents stated that her "entry date" was earlier. They were also reluctant to admit that Carol was the head teller and they argued that this designation had no meaning. They brought in all kinds of documents to prove that Carol made errors, although they also admitted that these errors were not serious enough to warrant discipline. They said that if they had had to make the choice just before Carol was elected union representative, they would have chosen to keep Carol.

Just before the hearings began, the bank's lawyer informed us that the bank would no longer offer Carol and Eileen temporary work, or first opportunity to be hired at the branch. The bank repeated this at the hearings, giving the picketting activities as the reason. We argued that the bank's withdrawal of the offers of employment because of the legitimate picket line simply proved our argument that their actions were consciously anti-union. We argued that Carol and Eileen were not acting disloyally, but were simply attempting to get the community to help them get their jobs back, and that their actions indicated their commitment to their jobs.

At the end of the hearing we were relieved, exhausted, and optimistic. The bank had clearly demonstrated their anti-union attitudes, and we had been able to cast doubt on the other possible reasons for Carol's termination.

For two and a half weeks we waited for the decision. This one was important to bank workers. Everyone was waiting to see whether the law really would protect our right to organize.

We were shocked when the Board ruled against us. They stated that we had failed to prove anti-union motivation was in the mind of the employer when Carol was laid off. It is impossible to prove conclusively what is in another person's mind. Motivation can only be indicated by circumstantial evidence, and our evidence had not convinced the Board. They had accepted the bank's statement that the layoffs were an economic necessity. Shortly after the decision came down, the number of bargaining unit positions in the branch was increased to five again, and one person had quit as expected. Our case was proved, but not until after the Board had ruled against us.

This decision by the Board would encourage banks to get rid of other union activists in like manner. We had to make the biggest possible fuss. We denounced it to the press, and wrote letters to everyone we could think of. The matter was raised in the House of Commons. It was front page headlines in the local Peninsula press.

We concluded we would have to try to enforce the law ourselves at Gibsons. The Gibsons experience would otherwise stand as a warning to bank workers—don't stand for union office or you'll lose your job; don't apply for certification or half your branch will be "laid off".

At National Executive meetings we had long discussions about legal strategy. We compared the Gibsons situation to Local 1's experiences in the restaurant industry. At Church's Chicken, union members had been harassed, intimidated and fired. We won a couple of unfair labour practice complaints but by that time it was too late. People were afraid of being fired. The fact that they had more than a 50% chance of getting their jobs back three months later was not incentive enough to be involved. Some withdrew from the union, others left Church's seeking better jobs. At Bimini, after putting so much effort into winning on the picket line, we lost at the Labour Relations Board. Two months after the strike ended, the scabs applied for decertification and the Board ordered a vote which we lost. We were amazed that the Board accepted the application for decertification so soon after the strike. This meant there was no incentive for employers to accept the union, to negotiate in good faith and then to attempt to make the collective agreement work. The Bimini decision encouraged employers to hold out through long strikes, and count on scabs and strikebreakers to decertify the union.

SORWUC members at Muckamuck restaurant were fighting the same management strategy that had defeated SORWUC at Church's. Union members were fired or had their hours cut so they were forced to quit. At meetings and informally we were looking for ways to defend our legal rights without expecting too much from the law.

We escalated our public campaign in Gibsons. We held bigger demonstrations at the bank branch every two weeks on Saturdays (the branch is open on Saturdays) all summer. We printed and distributed

posters, leaflets and bumper stickers urging everyone to boycott the branch. And we kept trying to resolve the issue at the bargaining table.

At each demonstration, there were speakers from other unions, and music. The turn-out ranged from thirty to 125. Lots of Local 1 members went from Vancouver by ferry each time, and trade unionists from Gibsons participated. We began a series of meetings with other trade unionists in Gibsons.

The Canadian Paperworkers Union donated the use of their hall, and made regular financial donations as well. The Fishermen's Union (UFAWU) were under attack by the federal government themselves. Nevertheless, they turned out to all our demonstrations and meetings, and donated money as well as time and effort. The Ferry Workers and the IWA also consistently supported the campaign. Carol did a lot of work in the community, speaking to senior citizens and other community groups as well as local unions. It was a good campaign. Our reports from members in other branches indicated that the campaign had been successful in cooling the anti-union behaviour of bank management elsewhere. They were taking us seriously.

In spite of our misgivings about the law, we had filed an unfair labour practice (before the Dulyk decision) saying that the withdrawal of the first opportunity of employment to Eileen was tantamount to firing for union activity. This complaint was settled without a hearing.

There's rumours of a walkout, rumours of a strike
Rumours of a picket, until the wages hike
But I've got this survival plan in case of storm and strife
Here's how I'll get the job done: I'll give it to my wife.
— "The Bosses' Lament" by T. Dash

14   Rumours of a Strike

Negotiating with the banks was a new experience for all of us. Sheree Butt, the Contract Committee representative for her branch, describes negotiations:

The first negotiating session with my employer, the Bank of Montreal, was in December, 1977. It was held at a fancy downtown hotel in Vancouver, which was to be our main meeting place for the next several months. The cost of all meeting rooms for negotiations was shared equally. The Bank of Montreal allowed unpaid time off for one employee from each of our twelve certified branches to attend negotiations. The bank workers were reimbursed for lost wages by the union.

Bank workers who had arrived from all over the province, met in the coffee shop to encourage each other and prepare for what was to follow. We then gathered up our contract proposals and headed up to the meeting room, anxious to arrive first so we could choose which side of the table to sit at.

Then, right on time, in walked five men, all dressed in three-piece business suits, each carrying a briefcase. They sat down, and proceeded to pull mounds of paper out of their briefcases. This went on for about five minutes before the meeting could begin. The bank's chief spokesperson introduced himself and the bank's committee. He was a labour relations specialist, formerly the Minister of Labour for Newfoundland and had been on the bank's payroll for five short weeks. The session started with him giving us a lecture on the whole bargaining process. We were told that there should be no pounding on the table, raising of voices, or exhausting marathon sessions.

They also asked that we make an agreement not to talk to the press during negotiations. We told them that we could make no such agreement. Of course we would not say anything to the press that could jeopardize negotiations, but we would use the press to inform bank workers and the public of our progress. Besides, we said, the press could sometimes be a useful tool in negotiations. They were furious. We were to find out through future meetings that they felt quite strongly about confidentiality. When we reprinted one of their letters in our "Weekly Bulletin" to union reps, they were outraged. They maintained that their correspondence should be a secret between themselves and the union office.

We raised the issue of joint bargaining with all the banks and referred to other industries in B.C. which negotiated jointly. The bank insisted on completing negotiations for one branch before proceeding to negotiate for the other eleven. They said they didn't mind if this procedure took a longer time. They chose to start with the Langley branch. We maintained that this contract would apply to all branches. When this negotiating session ended, we all walked away feeling excited, determined, bewildered and more than anxious to meet again to begin negotiating the contract we all hoped we would one day work under.

Our committee was different at each session. Of the twelve certified branches, usually five or six would be represented at the table. Some branches sent the same person each time for the sake of continuity. In others, union members took turns so more people could participate. We encouraged each other to speak up during meetings. Our negotiating committee knew a lot more about the bank than the industrial relations expert and personnel men. Our committee included tellers, control clerks, manager's secretaries, chief clerks and loans officers.

The Bank of Montreal often compared SORWUC to other unions, saying we were much more unreasonable than the OTEU and RCIU with whom they were also negotiating.

Maybe we were more determined because we worked in the industry every day. We knew how important the clauses that we drew up were. The Contract Committee had gone through an endless series of meetings to draw up proposals and go over arguments before negotiations began. Bank workers strongly defended the clauses in our proposals on working conditions. For example, our proposal on 'wickets' was: "All tellers shall be provided with chairs or stools. Tellers' wickets shall be designed and constructed in such a way that the employee can perform all regular duties while seated." Only a few credit unions and bank branches have wickets designed so that the tellers can work while seated. The banks provided stools but it is impossible to work from them. The banks' committees would get much more frustrated when an employee would argue one of the issues than if the union rep presented the arguments. The banks knew that a teller who arrived at negotiations after standing at her wicket all day could argue the 'wickets' clause better than anyone else. The bank workers who came to negotiations were the same ones who were involved in the contract committee meetings which drew up the proposals. We knew our stuff.

In our initial sessions with the Bank of Montreal, they refused to meet with us while employees from other banks were present. Charlotte (the UBW president) and the elected rep for part-time employees both worked at the Commerce. We could not allow the banks to tell us who could negotiate on our behalf. We referred the bank to a 1967 Ontario Labour Relations Board decision in which the Upholsterer's International Union charged Braemar Upholstered Furniture with failing to comply with the Ontario Labour Code by refusing to negotiate while certain members of the union's negotiating team was present until that person's eligibility was determined. The employer's objection was based on the fact that this individual was employed by a competing firm. The Board found that this did not disqualify the individual from attending negotiations. We initiated an unfair labour practice complaint against the Bank of Montreal. They finally agreed to recognize our entire Committee.

Our first meetings with the Commerce, Scotia, TD and Royal were similar to those of the Bank of Montreal, although each bank had its own way of dealing with us. The Scotia and the Royal had each hired lawyers to present the bank's position, while the Commerce and TD had "old-time bankers". The Bank of Montreal constantly bored us with long, philosophical speeches; the Commerce presented a relaxed, friendly front.

The Commerce refused to allow time off work for our committee members. We negotiated "on location" and all our meetings were held in the evening. Much time was spent discussing our "no discrimination" clause which all the banks hated. The Commerce's old time banker said that discrimination was definitely a thing of the past and that the clause was therefore unnecessary. A woman from our committee who had just left work one half hour earlier was outraged at this argument and said that male workers in her branch were allowed to smoke during office hours but women workers were under no circumstances allowed to. The bank spokesman turned to the branch manager, asked if this story was true and discovered that this was standard policy at that branch.

The same woman also described an earlier experience of discrimination. After working in the bank for several years, she had taken time off to have a child. When she applied to return to work at the Commerce, she was told at the interview that her child might keep her awake at night and she would be tired at work the next day. She was told to come back when the child was older!

Our negotiating meetings with the Royal were late in starting as they refused to meet with us until we had presented them with our completed contract proposals. Then they acted like they were doing us a favour by agreeing to negotiate before the Federal Court had ruled on their bargaining unit appeal. Our first meeting was in February and like the Bank of Montreal, held at an expensive Vancouver hotel. Since one of our Royal Bank certifications was in Kamloops, subsequent meetings were held at a hotel there. The Royal's committee never argued about where to meet, but they would allow only one employee time off work to attend negotiations. So we chose to meet in Kamloops after business hours to discuss the Kamloops branch, enabling all the members in that branch to come.

We would leave Vancouver early in the morning clutching suitcases and file folders for the seven hour drive to Kamloops in somebody's old car or on the bus. Reviewing last minute arguments, we would make our way to Kamloops.

At the beginning, Royal bank negotiations were a boost to our morale when contrasted with the other banks. Our initial meetings proceeded quite quickly and clarification of our proposals took only a few meetings. However, we were to learn through future meetings that the Royal was just as slow and unreasonable as the other banks.

At one Kamloops session, union members from the Bank of Montreal also attended. The Royal's negotiators refused to meet while the women from a "competing bank" were present. We argued for almost an hour but the bank was adamant. Since the meetings were so infrequent and involved so much travelling, we reluctantly agreed that the "competition" would leave. We continued the argument by mail using the same legal precedent that we used with the Bank of Montreal. The issue was never resolved with the Royal.

It took from February 13 to July 13, 1978, to initial three clauses: General Purpose, Union Bulletin Board, and Stewards. In July we held our first negotiating session for the Gibsons branch of the Royal. We agreed that each of the clauses we had initialled in Kamloops would also apply to the Gibsons branch.

Negotiations between SORWUC and the Scotia were an incredible test of our patience. Here the stalling tactics which all the banks used were the most obvious. Because we held certification for three branches, we were forced to clarify our proposals three times. The bank claimed this procedure was necessary so each branch manager could attend negotiations. We had to repeat everything three times for the benefit of the three managers. Each evening negotiations would be divided into three sessions. After the first explanation, their committee would adjourn, pack up all their gear and then reappear and reintroduce themselves accompanied by the new manager, to begin clarification of the same proposals. The same questions and the same arguments were repeated three times. They demanded a definition of almost every word in our proposals, and made every argument so technical and legalistic that the employees were first bewildered, then bored, then angry. It seemed we would never get to discuss any real issues. Bank managers rarely said a word at any of these meetings.

We protested the lack of progress in negotiations, suggesting that we meet more frequently. The Scotia refused to meet during the day as then their managers would have to leave the branch. They suggested meetings from seven to eleven thirty p.m. allotting one and a half hours for each branch. On September 26, 1977 we had given notice to bargain. In July 1978 we were still clarifying our proposals.

Our TD certification was one of our latest. We applied for certification for the branch in Tahsis on December 29, 1977. A small town with a population of approximately 1,600, Tahsis is situated on the west coast of Vancouver Island. The TD is the only bank in town. The Tahsis company sawmill is the town's main industry, the others are logging and fishing.

The bank announced that their employees in Tahsis would miss out on the regular cost of living increase plus a new northern allowance, the amount of which varied from one version to another but was generally believed to be about $1,000-$1,200 per year. This was similar to what the other banks were doing except that the TD did it to Tahsis employees before the certification even came through. This made it illegal, and we laid an unfair labour practice complaint. But for a while everyone believed that the main union organizer in the branch was responsible for them being $1,000 a year poorer. They all signed a letter withdrawing from the union. Then the bank appealed to the Federal Court of Appeal to try to have our certification overturned. They refused to negotiate with us while the appeal was pending. After we threatened to lay another unfair labour practice complaint, they finally agreed to negotiate.

Until then the bank workers in Tahsis were sure that the bank was winning. They were visited by management from Regional Office but never met any SORWUC members outside their own branch. Tahsis is isolated. It's not too far from Port McNeill but they haven't finished the road yet. One-way fare from Vancouver in a 10-seater Mallard aircraft is $65.00. Because of our financial state, many hours were spent travelling over old logging roads, by bus or hitch-hiking and enjoying scenic (but lengthy) boat trips.

As soon as the bank agreed to negotiate we held a meeting in Tahsis to finalize our proposals and signed up a majority again. The union had won a small victory by forcing the bank to negotiate. Tahsis is a union town and the bank workers were encouraged by friends and relatives. They were enraged at the difference between their wages and their lack of power compared to the mill workers. In spite of high turnover, it was not difficult to persuade new employees to join the union. We were always well represented at the bargaining sessions.

One thing that made the long trip worthwhile for the union representatives was the fact that the people of Tahsis were friendly to us and cool towards the bank's representatives. They weren't welcome in the pub, and looked uncomfortable in the coffee shop. The bank wanted to hold negotiations in the local hotel but there was a wildcat strike at the sawmill and the Tahsis Company got the only meeting room for their negotiations. Our negotiations were held in the bank branch.

Most of the time in negotiations we argued about grievances and unfair labour practices. We finally won the cost of living increase. We won some individual grievances and lost others. By July we had clarified some of the clauses in our proposals although nothing was agreed.

Each of the banks had presented us with pretty much the same proposals. Nothing in their proposals offered more (and in some cases, they offered less) than what non-union bank employees already received. The Bank of Montreal and the Royal had made a few minor concessions, but aside from those we had not won any of our demands in eight months of negotiations.

The banks were not taking us seriously, and were still actively working to undermine our support in the branches.

The Bank of Montreal received a report of an informal meeting at the West Vancouver branch. The bank circulated a memo to managers of certified branches. It was announced to employees that a strike vote had been conducted at the branch and that a strike had been unanimously rejected. We raised this issue at a negotiating session. The bank admitted it was a rumour but refused to accept statements by Jean and I, although we had both been present at the meeting, that there had

The Banks' Negotiating Committee

See no union; hear no union; say: "No union!"

been no vote of any kind taken. We demanded that a retraction of the bank's statement be circulated. In its usual pompous manner, the bank refused.

Even as we were sitting at the bargaining table, people were being fired. Carol and Eileen were fired from our Commerce branch in Gibsons. In March 1978 a union member was fired from a certified Vancouver branch of the Bank of Montreal and another union member was fired from our Bank of Montreal branch in Victoria. There were also firings at the TD in Tahsis and Gord Mullin, a union activist in a noncertified branch was fired by the Commerce.

Audrey had worked at the Bank of Montreal in Victoria for 15 years. After joining the union, she was first given two people's work to do and then asked to resign because they said she was too slow. She refused to resign and was fired. We decided against laying an unfair labour practice complaint in this case because the banks often get rid of women with many years of seniority whether or not they are union members. Instead, Audrey came to negotiations to express her outrage. At first the bank's negotiators said they knew nothing about the firing and said the bank must have had a good reason for it. Audrey attended several more negotiating sessions without positive results. She then grieved her firing through the bank's grievance procedure to no avail.

The UBW Contract Committee, with representatives from each of our twenty-three certified branches, continued to meet regularly. Each meeting heard reports on all our negotiations with the different banks. The Committee was responsible for carrying out the decisions we had made at our contract conferences in the fall. We had set out to negotiate a master agreement for the banking industry in B.C. At the time of the conferences, the UBW was signing up 100 new members each month. Now we found ourselves negotiating for twenty-three isolated branches out of about 800 branches in B.C.

The kinds of provisions we wanted, covering seniority, transfers and promotions, just couldn't be achieved in one branch of the TD, or two branches of the Royal, or even twelve branches of the Bank of Montreal. The banks were outraged at our attempts to negotiate provisions that would affect branches that weren't certified. We came up with various compromises, but we were frustrated by the impossibility of the whole situation.

In terms of day-to-day negotiations, the Committee had eventually divided into one committee for each bank. Our objective was still to achieve a master contract, but we realized that in these negotiations we would have to get the best we could out of each bank.

Reports of Contract Committee Meetings and negotiating sessions were mailed to members regularly. We wanted discussion and feedback from members in non-certified as well as certified branches. We were trying to use our proposals and the banks' responses to build the organizing campaign.

After several months of arguments and meetings, we were desperate about our lack of progress. In our negotiations with the Scotia, we hadn't even clarified half of our contract proposals. Much of the discussion in the union now centred around conciliation.

We invited Tom McGrath from Local 400 of the Canadian Brotherhood of Railway, Transport & General Workers (Seamen's Section) to speak to the Contract Committee about his union's experience with the conciliation process. Either side can ask the federal Minister of Labour to appoint a conciliation officer to assist in negotiations. The officer has no power to make recommendations binding on the parties. His role is to encourage a voluntary settlement. Under federal labour law, the conciliation process is a legal requirement before a union can go on strike. In May 1978 we decided to apply for conciliation for the Bank of Montreal, the Commerce and the Scotia.

The banks were hysterical when we told them that we had applied for conciliation. They said that our actions were premature, that everything was going smoothly, and there was no need for third party intervention. They seemed very nervous.

Not long after the conciliation officers were appointed we realized we had built up false hope. We were hoping that the officers would be successful in making more headway than we were able to, but soon began considering the conciliation process a prelude to a strike.

When Linda first talked to the conciliation officer about the Scotia negotiations, he made it quite clear that he did not want to meet in the evenings and that the infrequency of our meetings was ridiculous. He said he would call up the bank and demand we meet more often and during office hours. After talking with the Scotia's officers, he called back to say he was unable to get the bank to meet on his (and our) terms. If the conciliation officers couldn't even get the banks to meet more often, how could they get the banks to negotiate seriously?

The banks were mainly interested in stalling negotiations and depleting our limited resources by tedious branch-bargaining. The wages of workers in certified branches were still frozen. Other bank workers were convinced to "wait and see" how the union did in negotiations. Time was on the side of the banks.

The UBW Saskatchewan branches were also in negotiations and were running up against similar problems. Jean Burgess from Saskatchewan describes their negotiations:

Our first bargaining session with the Royal Bank in Melfort took place on February 28th, 1978. The meeting had been a show of power. The Royal had tried to postpone it because their negotiator was on a sailing holiday. We were not sympathetic and demanded that they meet within thirty days as was required in the Canada Labour Code. (We were carrying the Code around with us in those days.) They finally conceded and sent along their top man in charge of union matters and a representative from Head Office and Regional Office. We had booked a room in a building on the fairgrounds at the edge of town. The building was an uninsulated aluminum shed in the middle of a field. A noisy fan blew hot air around the room. A bare light bulb hung down over the table and folding straight chairs. We liked the place because it was cheap, and had a big kitchen with a phone (for emergency calls to our support people). The kitchen was a perfect place to caucus and we planned to do a lot of that.

When we had previously tried to protest our working conditions, we couldn't even get a personnel officer from Regional Office to come and see us, but now that we had formed a union we had bigwigs from Montreal sitting in the fairgrounds listening to what we wanted.

We felt both nervous and determined when we first met. We raised our concern that the negotiating committee members from the branch be able to have time off work. We were still arguing this issue at 4:00 p.m. when in walked seven bank workers from the branch. Management hadn't known who was behind the union and when our committee had first sat down they had eagerly written down all our names. But when seven more people walked in their jaws hit the table. We caucused in the kitchen and hugged each other. Until that moment we had not been sure of our support. Tension was high in the branch and we had had no idea who would come to that first negotiating session. We went back to the table and presented our proposals. After all the trouble in the branch, this was a day of victory for us.

We were forced to agree that only one person would be allowed time off work without pay to negotiate. It was also agreed that the bank would be given one weeks notice as to who the person would be. One day the branch manager told Pat, who was to attend negotiations that day, that she was needed at work and we would have to send someone else. They could not decide who would be on our bargaining committee. We went to the table without Pat, but refused to bargain or discuss anything. The bank representatives had come all the way from Montreal and though we wouldn't leave the table, we refused to talk about anything. We pulled out our notebooks and our contracts and silently went to work writing up our arguments for various contract clauses. Not a word was spoken for four hours. There were some red and purple faces on the other side of the table as we serenely went about our work. Pat arrived at 4:00 p.m. and we called a supper break. At the evening session we got an agreement from the Bank that they would not interfere with who we wanted at the bargaining table. The afternoon of silence had been worth it.

Our union meetings changed from general complaint sessions about working conditions to intense, productive work sessions on contract proposals. The bank's strategy seemed to be to stall the negotiations as much as they could. They demanded "clarification" of each clause before they would begin bargaining. It was only when we were able to show some collective strength that we made any gains.

We learned the power of publicity. Melfort is a small town. The Royal Bank occupies an old stone building in the centre of town. From the front of the bank you can see all of the downtown area. Handing out union leaflets to customers at the door of the bank is not a common occurrence. We explained that the bank was stalling in negotiations and we told them about our grievances and our demands. People were very supportive. Management never said a word about our leafletting, but they were surprisingly agreeable to a number of items that we had been negotiating for months.

We began thinking about what a strike would mean. We had learned a lot since our first decision to organize. We had helped in a small way to support the dairy workers' strike in Melfort. We had visited their picket line, and walked and talked with them about their union concerns. They extended to us congratulations for unionizing in the bank. Some women in Melfort printed our first leaflet and helped hand it out at the bank. We realized community support was essential.

The Bank was trying to outwait us. Three of our negotiators in Melfort were pregnant and management figured that when they had their babies they would be gone for good. Not so. All three women soon returned to the negotiating table. Negotiations were going poorly. We decided to apply for conciliation, despite management's insistence that negotiations were moving along smoothly.

The bank's stalling and the wage freeze were taking their toll on our support in the branch and the CLC unions were helping us less and less. We went to a union meeting in Prince Albert. The workers there were mostly women and worked in a nursing home. They encouraged us to speak about the problems of working in the bank. They were appalled by our wages. They voiced their support for our struggle and said they would try to help. At the end of the meeting, the president (who was the only man in the room) indicated that times were tough all over, but that the CLC, to which they were affiliated, was organizing the banks. We left the meeting knowing that we had the support of the general membership but not the president. We received no donations from them.

But the banks are made of marble
With a guard at every door
And the vaults are stuffed with silver
That the workers sweated for.
— "The Banks are Made of Marble",
a traditional labour song

15 Withdrawal from Negotiations

After eight months of futile negotiations, we began talking about strikes. Although we had been hopeful the conciliation process would avert a strike, we knew we had to discuss an alternative action if it didn't.

The banks seemed prepared to sign a contract that would be basically the same as present bank policy and benefits; we needed a contract that could be used as a tool for future organizing. A poor contract would not encourage unorganized bank workers to join the union. Bank management could use such a contract as another argument against further organizing.

Bank workers agreed that a strike would be the only way we could force our employers to sign the kind of contract we deserved—one that would recognize our skills, responsibility and seniority. The first question was—which bank, and where, would we strike? It was decided to conduct strike votes at Commerce branches. Secret ballot votes were taken by members in early July at three of our five certified Commerce branches. (Langley, Port McNeill and Gibsons). Each voted 100% in favour of striking. Our strategy was to strike one or more branches and build a province-wide boycott of the Commerce in support of the strike. Port McNeill, a union town, would most likely have been the choice of where to strike.

We knew that a strike would probably last a long time. We expected the bank to bring in scabs from Regional Office or other branches as closing the branch would mean conceding victory to us. They could continue to operate behind a picket line, but many of their customers wouldn't cross. However, the strike would also be expensive for us. We voted to pay strike pay of at least $500 per month for each striker and would coordinate publicity for the provincial boycott of other Commerce branches.

The UBW had no strike fund. We expected to get the money from trade unionists and other bank workers. Realizing that the strike would not be just for those Commerce employees on the picket line but would affect all bank workers in B.C., some members agreed to contribute a small portion of their pay to the strike fund. To provide subsistence for those on strike, we needed pledges of at least $3,000 per month.

The success of the strike would depend on the boycott campaign. The bank could afford to lose business at one branch for years, but we were confident we could significantly reduce their profits for the whole province. We would need a lot of help in such a campaign. The support from the trade union movement had been decreasing. This was partly because of the CLC's campaign against us. But it was also because of our recent lack of success in organizing. Surely the first bank strike in B.C. history should win the active support of the whole trade union movement to make the boycott a success (accounts withdrawn, strike pay pledged, leaflets handed out).

In the long run though, the future of the UBW depended on the organizing drive. We had to consider the effect of a boycott on bank workers. Could we really set up information pickets outside those Commerce branches where we had no members or supporters? As we would be asking customers to withdraw their accounts, the bank could use our boycott as an excuse for layoffs to turn bank workers against the union. If we had had more members we might have been able to use the boycott to build the union. But in most branches there would be no union members to answer the arguments put forward by management.

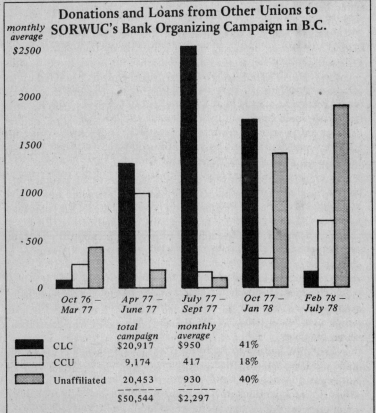

Donations and Loans from Other Unions to SORWUC's Bank Organizing Campaign in B.C.

monthly average

		total campaign	monthly average	
◼ (black)	CLC	$20,917	$950	41%
☐ (white)	CCU	9,174	417	18%
▨ (shaded)	Unaffiliated	20,453	930	40%
		$50,544	$2,297	

Although the CLC represents approximately 70.9% of union members in B.C., donations from CLC affiliates amounted to less than half of total donations from unions to our organizing campaign. From January 1978, our expenses increased dramatically (lost wages and travel for negotiations, two new salaries for UBW organizers). At the same time, donations, particularly from CLC affiliates, declined.

The UBW had scheduled a strike strategy conference for Sunday, July 23, 1978. The night before the conference, we organized an informal meeting of all members of the UBW, Local 1 and National Executives as well as the UBW delegates who were in town for the next day's strike conference. Whatever the UBW decided to do would affect the union as a whole and we wanted to hear the views of Local 1 members. The disastrous financial situation of the UBW could also mean that Local 1 would also be pulled under. (They did pay some of our bills.) Local 1 was involved in new organizing in restaurants, offices and trust companies, and still on strike at the Muckamuck Restaurant.

That night and the next day we went over and over the serious problems we were faced with, trying to find a solution. The banks' eighteen or so appeals to the Federal Courts and their insistence on branch by branch bargaining had had the desired effect. We had run out of money and were overwhelmed by debts. As our expenses increased because of negotiations, the amount of money coming in from other unions had declined.

Dodie and Sheree had to be laid off by the UBW and Jean by the National. We would be trying to negotiate twenty-four branch agreements without even one paid representative. We were three months behind in our rent. Thousands of dollars in other debts had piled up, as well as our $30,000 legal bill. We could no longer afford the cost of travelling expenses and lost wages to have bank workers attend negotiations. We did not have the support of enough bank workers to conduct an effective strike and could not get a good contract without one. Our organizing drive had come to a halt; we hadn't signed up a significant number of bank workers in months.

The CLC had been actively campaigning against us for some time. Affiliated unions and labour councils had been instructed not to give money to SORWUC. Bill Smalley, a CLC rep, debated with Jackie at a meeting of Local 213 of the International Brotherhood of Electrical Workers. Against his instructions, the membership voted to give $300 to the UBW. But in most locals we didn't even get the opportunity to answer the CLC.

The CLC refused to consider even sharing the cost of the legal expenses of the branch by branch decision. Since the decision was being appealed by the Royal Bank, we asked the CLC for financial help in view of the fact that their certifications would also be wiped out if the bank was successful. Again, their answer was no.

That UBW meeting on July 23 was the most difficult and depressing conference we ever had. We couldn't continue to negotiate and we couldn't go on strike.

The conference passed the following recommendations to be proposed to the UBW membership:

That SORWUC stop negotiating on a branch basis, effective immediately;

That SORWUC continue to support members in certified and non-certified branches, and invite them to remain members and continue to organize;

That SORWUC would not stand in the way of its certified branches joining another union.

Bank workers present at the meeting were extremely upset but agreed with the recommendations as we all realized that our employers had successfully won this round. We decided to allow ourselves, and all UBW members, another week to come up with a solution. There would be another conference of bank employees the following weekend to make a final decision.

During the week, meetings were held throughout the province with members at certified branches to talk to them about the state of our union and to try to come up with an alternate course of action. As well, we phoned members all over B.C.

The meeting on July 30th ratified the votes taken the previous week. Some bank workers, but very few, were against the decision. Mostly bank workers were upset, furious, depressed and demoralized. We all cried for days. It was the most difficult union decision we had ever made.

We now had to inform every single SORWUC member, our supporters and other trade unionists. Hundreds of letters of explanation went out.

The public announcement was made Monday, July 31, at 1:00 p.m. Newscasters and reporters packed into our union office to hear Charlotte Johnson and Jackie Ainsworth release our statement.

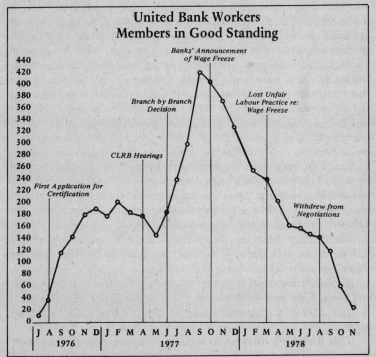

Note: The most members in good standing from July '76 to Nov. '78 was 422. But during the same period, we signed up a total of 733 bank workers.

This press release outlined the major reasons for the bank workers' decision to withdraw from negotiations. While we pointed out the many anti-union tactics of the banks and described negotiations as a farce, much emphasis was put on the role of the CLC. "The lack of support from the CLC has hindered our campaign as much as the anti-union actions of the banks. As long as most unions in British Columbia continue to kowtow to the CLC executive, thousands of workers will remain unorganized. The CLC and its affiliates must take responsibility for that."

We explained that we had begun discussing strike strategy and "it was at that point that we realized we cannot take on the banks without full moral and financial support of the trade unionists in this province."

We outlined the problems we faced with the banks. "In terms of negotiations, our backs were against the wall and we had no other choice except to go on strike or sign a lousy contract." We described the many hostile actions of our employers such as their anti-union meetings in the branches, the withholding of wages and benefits from certified branches and their continual attempts to fire union members. We pointed out that we were not giving up, but pulling out of the first round and concentrating on building the bargaining power necessary to compel the banks to sign the type of union contract bank workers deserved.

Following our press conference, we were on national news for three consecutive nights. Almost every time we turned on the radio, we heard one of us making a statement. We were overwhelmed by the number of phone calls and requests for interviews. While we knew the importance of following up and keeping the issue in the media, we were exhausted, demoralized and frustrated. When one TV program invited the UBW to appear for a telephone debate with a CLC representative, no one wanted to go. Dodie, Sheree and Linda finally agreed. It turned out to be a good show and gave us an opportunity to debate publicly with the CLC.

Following the initial publicity and mailings to members and supporters, there was one very important thing yet to do—explain to the bank workers who had not joined the union.

We were sure that in branches where there were no union members, management would be criticizing the union. Bank workers were hearing only their managers' versions of how SORWUC went broke and was now defunct.

We wrote up a leaflet explaining the events which led to our decision, and made a final appeal to the thousands of bank employees who hadn't joined the union.

Once again we were able to mobilize hundreds of wonderful leafletters to assist in the mass distribution of this leaflet. Bank branches in most areas of B.C. were leafletted during the next couple of weeks.

Upon release of our initial statement, we began to hear criticisms. SORWUC was accused of abandoning bank workers and 'leaving them out on a limb'. The CLC executive publicly stated that our decision might have serious repercussions and that active union members in the banks could be fired. We explained that it is illegal to fire anyone for trade union activity whether in a certified or non-certified branch, and that we would continue to protect our members.

As well, we were approached by leaders of other unions who wanted us to "turn over" our twenty-four certifications to them. Needless to say, we did not agree. Legally, one union can't just hand over a group of employees to another union. It would be clearly undemocratic for bank workers who had joined an independent Canadian union to suddenly find themselves in some big international through no choice of their own. The option for bank workers to join another union of their choice was open to them when their SORWUC certification was cancelled. Only one of our twenty-four branches chose to join another union, the CLC's Union of Bank Employees.

We decided that although we had lost the first round, we would continue as the UBW Section of SORWUC and prepare for our second campaign. Afterwards it seemed we had always known that an industry as large as the banking industry would not crack at the first assault. The difficult part was figuring out when to end the first assault, pull back and prepare for the second.

Our decision to withdraw from negotiations was a serious setback for our members in Saskatchewan. It weakened their morale and their position at the bargaining table.

The Saskatchewan UBW faced many of the same problems we had in B.C. Both the TD and the Royal were stalling in negotiations and there had been no new organizing for months.

However, the members in Saskatchewan decided to continue to negotiate in spite of the decision in B.C. They went the whole route provided by the Canada Labour Code: first a conciliation officer, then a conciliation commissioner. All to no avail. The commissioner's report on the TD in Regina recommended a settlement with no improvement in wages, hours or vacations. He proposed that loans officers should not be covered by the contract, even though the union had fought successfully to have the Board include them in the bargaining unit. We could hardly believe that a neutral, government-appointed commissioner recommended a settlement with no monetary improvements.

The choice for these two branches was to sign a bad contract or go on a prolonged strike. Neither felt they could win a strike, isolated as it would be from most bank employees in Saskatchewan and, given the union's worsening relationship with the CLC, from the rest of the labour movement. Neither group wanted to sign a bad contract.

In the spring of 1979, the units decided to withdraw from negotiations.

Whatever will they do
Whatever on this earth
When all us working women
Demand what we are worth?
—chorus of "The Bosses' Lament"
by T. Dash

16   The Balance Sheet

In 1978, there weren't enough bank workers in the UBW to win the union contracts we deserve. But we know now what we're up against, and we know it can be done. In August 1976, many bank workers thought it was against the law to organize a union in the banks. Now we know that when we have confidence in ourselves and our co-workers and the courage to stand up for our rights, we will have the power to win the respect we deserve.

Throughout our campaign, we kept running up against the same old myths about women and about unions. Most bank workers, like other unorganized workers, find out about unions from the media. The banks encourage us to accept the common myths: the union is a "third party" interfering in the relationship between workers and employers; unions have too much power; workers never make up the wages they lose in strikes; a union contract means unnecessary and unreasonable rules; unions order people out on strike; it's impossible for a small independent union to take on corporations as large as the banks.

It is a farce to think we are negotiating as individuals with the banks. Our campaign showed that by acting collectively as a union of bank workers we can establish a new relationship between ourselves and our employers. Our contract proposals were written by bank workers and we did not demand unnecessary rules. We demanded protection from arbitrary management action and bureaucratic inaction.

We learned that most unions are required by law and by their own constitutions to conduct membership strike votes before striking, that most unions hold membership votes to ratify collective agreements before they are signed with the employer and that the workers who are prepared to strike are those who have the best pay and working conditions. The legal right to strike is an important equalizer in employer-employee relations. This right allows employees to sit down at a negotiating table with a substantial degree of the economic power that the employer has already. It is true that strikers lose wages during a strike, but from a simple dollars and cents point of view strikes can pay. Unionized cashiers in supermarkets, who have been on strike a few times in B.C., and have threatened strike action more often, could go on strike for an average of four months a year and still make a higher annual wage in the remaining eight months than bank tellers get paid in an entire year. Even with loss of wages during strikes, they are clearly better off than workers who do not have the right to strike.

The problem is not that unions are too big and powerful; the problem is that the majority of workers are still unorganized and therefore powerless. When the trade union movement represents most working people, instead of a minority, it will be possible to overcome the divisions between workers. We can then deal with general social questions that can't be solved within a single workplace or industry, like child care, health care, pollution, education.

Other unions also started small, and SORWUC's campaign in the banks is not unusual in labour history. When other industries were organized for the first time, new independent unions were built. The tradesmen's unions fifty years ago said industrial workers could not be organized. Today, many trade unionists say women workers are unorganizable. Major organizing campaigns have always involved shake-ups in the established unions of the time.

"Organizing unions is something men do, not women." This myth is tied to a lot of other myths: women only work temporarily, until we get married and have families; it is right and proper that women earn less than men; women should not be interested in work or unions; it is not feminine to fight back; we will be rescued from the bank by rich husbands; men are the breadwinners and women are working for pin money. Bank workers can't win ordinary union benefits without challenging these myths.

We know our work is important and we take pride in our skills. We don't have to accept being treated like part of the decor, subject to arbitrary management-imposed dress codes. At one data centre we were told we could wear blue jeans so long as they didn't have back pockets. One branch manager said, "There's no way I would let my daughter wear a denim skirt and I won't have it worn in my branch." Dress codes vary from branch to branch and from manager to manager. We don't have to accept such humiliating treatment. We don't have to accept a compliment from the boss, or a gold star on a teller's blotter, as compensation for unpaid overtime and a substitute for a raise.

Our employers point to the few women managers and tell us that if we compete with each other, we can get ahead in the banks as individuals. Because there are no rules governing promotions and transfers, our desire to improve our wages and working conditions reinforces our dependence on our bosses. If the accountant or manager likes you, you may have a chance at a better job. But don't be too conscientious—you may make yourself indispensable as a teller.

Those of us who are older know from personal experience that women spend most of our lives in the work force, and no one is going to rescue us. We have the most to gain from the job security and seniority rights in a union contract, and because of our knowledge of the industry, we have an important contribution to make to the union. But we are afraid that we could be suddenly found incompetent and replaced with younger, more decorative and lower paid newcomers. We are encouraged to see our co-workers as a threat to our jobs. The banks try to use our fears to turn us against the union.

Bank workers in the union learned a new respect for ourselves and our co-workers and overcame many of the divisions fostered by management. We had been encouraged to blame ourselves or our co-workers when we worked late night after night. Through our union meetings we found out how general this problem was. In negotiations we demanded that the banks provide an adequate training program for new tellers and hire enough employees in each branch to do the work without overtime. In some branches tellers and ledgerkeepers had been blaming data centre employees for extra work and data centre employees complained about the branches. For many of us, the union meetings were the first opportunity we ever had to compare our working conditions, and those discussions opened our eyes to how much we had in common and how much we could gain by working together.

We had been blaming ourselves for our lousy wages. After all, we are "just tellers", "just bank workers", "just women". Management told us to keep our paycheques secret, hoping to convince us to see our low pay as an individual problem. Single parents who couldn't make ends meet were supposed to see this as a personal failure. At the UBW contract conferences, we worked out a budget for a worker with one dependent child and realized that we couldn't possibly live on our present wages without going into debt. We discussed our wages frankly, and put them in their historical context. Early in this century, when bank tellers were men and construction labourers had no unions, bank tellers made fifty per cent more than construction labourers. Now bank tellers are women and the union rate for construction labourers is twice what we make. The reason our skills aren't recognized or paid for is because we're women, and we're unorganized.

There are now many bank workers who are experienced union organizers. We formed our own local and ran our own meetings, wrote leaflets, presented cases to the Labour Relations Board, and negotiated with our employers. All this experience will go into building a strong organization of bank workers. But thousands of bank workers decided to wait and see what would happen to the union before they committed themselves. A union in the banks will only become a reality when thousands of bank employees join. Our strength depends on the decision of every bank worker individually. We hope that this book will help our co-workers take stock, assess what was accomplished and imagine what can happen when they join us.

All bank workers benefitted from the campaign. When the SORWUC drive began, bank workers in Greater Vancouver started at $600 per month or less, and the average wage for a teller was $636 per month. According to the Vancouver Sun, July 4, 1979, bank tellers received the largest pay increase of any category of clerical workers in 1978—15.4%. The average wage for tellers is now $885 per month. All banks introduced dental plans, and there are no longer deductions from tellers' wages to cover cash shortages. The Commerce has instituted regular coffee breaks and pays overtime on a daily basis. The Bank of Montreal has a job posting system in some districts. Several banks have improved vacations. These changes resulted from the union scare; imagine what we could win if we could threaten strike.

We still earn much less than the average B.C. wage ($1,381 per month). Our seniority is not recognized in relation to transfers, promotions or job security. There is no effective grievance procedure. And bank workers will fall behind again if the banks believe that the threat of unionization is past.

We are in a better position to fight than we were. SORWUC as a whole has grown in numbers and experience. The formation of Local 3 (Oxfam employees) means we now have members from coast to coast. The Muckamuck Restaurant strike, over a year long, has shown that our union can withstand a long battle, and can raise strike pay when we need it. The UBW continues to meet as a Section of SORWUC. We are fighting unfair labour practice complaints on behalf of our members. Although many feared that union organizers would be blacklisted by the banks, Dodie, Sheree and Eileen Quigley are all back working in the industry. Jackie is still at Victory Square and is back in the ledger department. Dodie got her job as part of the settlement of an unfair labour practice complaint. When Eileen was hired, the interviewer looked at her letter from the Commerce saying her work was satisfactory and she had been laid off due to a shortage of work. He said, "Since when has the Commerce started laying off employees?" She explained it was a new branch that wasn't doing very well. "I've never heard of that before." Eileen wished the Board had been there.

Our campaign showed we don't need a lot of money to organize the banks. Our financial crisis was more a symptom than a cause. When we have a thousand members in B.C. banks, our own union dues will cover basic expenses of a provincial campaign.

We will continue to need the support of other unions. Members of other unions played an important role in encouraging bank workers during the first drive. They learned from us about the problems of organizing unorganized industries and we learned from their union experience. But as the financial donations from unions declined, so did the moral support. Building a new union in an unorganized industry, we were bound to face incredible hassles on the job. We should not also have to take on the labour movement. But the established unions have not been involved in major organizing campaigns for decades, the structure of the CLC is not geared to organizing, and many men trade unionists are not yet convinced that women should earn wages comparable to theirs, or that their wives should spend evenings and weekends at union meetings. This situation could not be changed overnight, but we did win many supporters who will be there when we need them in our second assault on the banks.

The UBW campaign cleared up the basic legal questions. The banks either lost or withdrew all their appeals of CLRB decisions to the federal court. The Board's decisions to include managers' secretaries, loans officers and part-time employees in the bargaining unit, as well as the decision that a branch is a unit, have been tested in court. That's one set of problems we won't have to deal with in the next campaign. The

federal Labour Code has been amended to remove a few of the difficulties we encountered in the first drive. We have established that it
is possible for bank workers to organize and we have learned not to put
too much faith in the laws and the Board's enforcement of them. We
have to rely on our own strength, with the support of other trade
unionists and the community as a whole.

Our employers are among the most profitable corporations in this
country, and their profits depend on us. The banks are the biggest
private employers of women. Once we are united, a union of bank
employees will have enormous power. There are tens of thousands of us.
A bank workers' union will have locals in cities, towns and villages right
across the country, and bank workers will be a force in our communities. Bank workers organized will have the power to win decent wages,
job security and dignity on our jobs. Our victories will benefit all
working women in this country.

Appendix : Correspondence Between SORWUC and the CLC, 1977

Letter to CLC from SORWUC
July 5, 1977

Urgent Financial Appeal
Donald Montgomery
Secretary-Treasurer
Canadian Labour Congress

Dear Brother Montgomery:

In June the Canada Labour Relations Board handed down an historic decision. It reversed a 1959 decision and made it possible to organize banks branch by branch.

Our Union and the Canadian Union of Bank Employees in Ontario, two small independent unions, successfully argued for branch by branch certification although larger and more established unions had said that the CLRB would never accept this position. Our legal expenses for the precedent-setting decision will amount to over $10,000.

Our Union has now applied for over 20 bank branches including a data centre and we are engaged in a province-wide organizing drive. In order to organize the province we need a minimum $5000 per month operating budget.

Less than 1% of workers in the finance industry are unionized. The average starting wage in banks in B.C. is less than half the average B.C. wage. Over 80% of women in banks are clerical workers; 80% of men in banks are management. Our Union was formed to organize the unorganized particularly in industries where women are concentrated—the industries where established unions have had the least success.

Since our first application for certification in August 1976 the response from bank employees across B.C. has been tremendous. We have the enthusiasm and the organizers to organize the province, but we are in urgent need of financial assistance. We are asking your organization for a substantial contribution. If you wish, we would be pleased to meet with you to discuss any questions you might have.

Enclosed are highlights of the CLRB decision, and our latest leaflet.
In solidarity,
Elizabeth Godley
National Secretary
SORWUC

Letter to SORWUC from CLC
July 19, 1977

Dear Sister Godley:

This will acknowledge receipt of your letter dated July 5th in which you make a brief report on the organizing activities of your union in the province of British Columbia. It appears that your campaign has been given a lift with the recent decision of the Canada Labour Relations Board, and has also created a national interest as the Canadian Labour Congress Regional Offices across the country are receiving calls daily from bank employees seeking information on the progress of organizing campaigns in their area.

The Congress has been holding discussions with the small independent "Canadian Union of Bank Employees" which has had some organizing success in south western Ontario. This organization also reports increased interest among bank employees in that part of the country. All these are most encouraging signs and it is imperative that organizing drives afford the workers the opportunity to become members of the union of their choice.

Your request that the Canadian Labour Congress make a special contribution to help defray the organizing expenses of your union will be placed before the next meeting of the Executive Council of the CLC and I will contact you as soon as a decision is reached by that Council.

Fraternally yours,
Donald Montgomery
Secretary-Treasurer

Letter to CLC from SORWUC
July 25, 1977

Brothers and Sisters:

We must protest the action of the Office and Technical Employees Union (Office and Professional Employees International Union) in mailing leaflets to bank branches in B.C. It is not surprising that this literature has been used by management personnel in their campaign to encourage bank employees to withdraw from membership in our union.

Our small union took on a task which the OTEU said was impossible. We carried out the groundwork, achieving a favourable decision from the Canada Labour Relations Board, at great expense, and building an organization of bank employees over 400 strong. And now, the OTEU begins a campaign to organize bank employees in B.C.

In the U.S., where the OPEIU is based, the proportion of working women who are union members has declined from 17% in 1950 to 12.5% in 1976. The overwhelming majority of clerical workers in the private sector in Canada are still unorganized. Surely the OTEU could spend its money on organizing the unorganized in the U.S., or elsewhere in Canada, rather than mailing leaflets to bank managers in B.C.

If our organizing campaign is to be successful, we need support from organized labour. We would like to renew our request for a meeting with you to discuss this further.

Yours sincerely,
Jean Rands
National President
copies sent to: B.C. Federation of Labour, OTEU Locals 15 and 378, Vancouver

Letter to SORWUC from CLC
September 13, 1977

Dear Sister Rands:

This will acknowledge receipt of your correspondence dated July 25, 1977 concerning the actions of the Office and Professional Employees International Union.

This Congress is cognizant of the progress made by your organization and the dedication of individuals that made it possible. We sincerely hope that the lack of finances, staff and affiliation to a stronger back-up organization will not impede your progress and that your members, present or in the future, will not be placed at a disadvantage due to these impediments.

With respect to the actions of the Office and Professional Employees International Union in British Columbia, you must understand that this organization is an affiliate of the Congress and has a long history of organizing employees in the banking and finance industry.

If an official of the Office and Professional Employees Union made the statement that organizing bank employees was impossible, I am not aware of it. What I am aware of is the fact that the Office and Professional Employees International Union obtained the first certification for bank employees. This certification was on behalf of employees of the Montreal and District Savings Bank. In addition, the Office and Professional Employees International Union presently holds bargaining rights for one hundred and thirty nine units in the banking and finance industries and these units are covered by thirty-five collective agreements.

I want to assure you that I don't wish to deprecate in any way what your organization claims to have accomplished by way of certification by the Canada Labour Relations Board, however, I would be remiss if I did not mention the fact that this Congress has spent much time, effort and money in pressing to have removed the impediments which act as an effective barrier for workers to join unions and the certification of bank workers units, irrespective of union affiliation, is a natural outgrowth of our efforts in this regard.

In closing, I must state that the Office and Professional Employees International Union as an affiliate of this Congress is entitled to our full support in their efforts to organize within their jurisdiction and we are co-operating with them.

If your organization wishes to enter into serious discussions with a view to entering the main stream of labour, our staff would be happy to discuss the possibilities with you.

With best regards, I remain,

Sincerely yours,

Joe Morris, President

Letter to CLC from SORWUC
October 6, 1977

Dear Brother Morris:

Thank you for your letter of September 13, 1977.

We are grateful for your words of encouragement. But we are surprised that you object to our taking credit for the CLRB decision allowing branch by branch certification of banks. Since SORWUC is responsible for the legal costs of the decision, it is only natural that we would also take credit for it. Prior to the decision, representatives of the CLC and Office and Professional Employees International Union told us we were wasting time and money taking an application for a single branch unit to the Canada Labour Relations Board. Fortunately, we disregarded this advice and won the favourable decision.

We are pleased that the Congress is cognizant of the progress made by our organization, and that you propose that we enter into serious discussions with you. In the past, we have been told that we could become part of the CLC only by dissolving our organization or merging with an already existing affiliate, or perhaps by becoming a directly chartered local of the CLC.

We are not interested in any of the above options. If we were assured of substantial financial support, our National Executive would be prepared to recommend to our members that SORWUC affiliate to the CLC *as a national organization.* SORWUC has spent five years leafletting, holding meetings with workers in the finance, service and retail industries, organizing small units and negotiating collective agreements—slowly building the framework of a union which is capable of organizing unorganized working women. Our members assisted the organization of two thousand workers into the Association of University and College Employees, also mostly women. SORWUC members have the most experience in the kind of organization required to unionize the finance industry. Financial assistance from the CLC would speed up the process. A regular budget would remove a great deal of worry. But SORWUC has survived the first five years, and we expect the next five will be less difficult.

We do appreciate the accomplishments of the trade union movement. Working women formed SORWUC precisely because we wanted the benefits of unionization. But the established unions have not been able to meet the needs of unorganized women in the private sector. As you know, there is a rapid decline in the number of women union members in the United States. If your international affiliates are incapable of organizing women workers in their own country, why should we expect that they can do the job in Canada? In British Columbia, a majority of women union members are in unions not affiliated to the CLC or the AFL - CIO. Consequently, SORWUC does not feel isolated from the "main stream of labour". We do not make independence a principle; however, we are determined to run our own affairs.

In regard to the so-called organizing efforts of the Office and Professional Employees International Union, we think this organization is more concerned with undermining SORWUC's efforts than with organizing bank workers. Since the June decision allowing branch by branch certification, the OPEIU has applied for certification for only two branches, both in B.C. The only application by a CLC affiliate outside B.C. was by the United Steelworkers of America. If the OPEIU is so interested in organizing banks, why is it not applying for branches in Toronto, where there is the greatest concentration of bank workers in all of

Canada; and why is it not applying for bank branches in Quebec, where it already has a base in the Montreal City and District Savings bank?

The effect of the entry of the OPEIU into bank organizing in B.C. has been to undermine, not strengthen, the attempts by bank workers to gain union representation. Anti-union management and supervisory employees now argue that bank workers should check out the other union before joining SORWUC. Of course, these people are not OPEIU supporters. They are using the presence of another union as an excuse to delay unionization. We believe the actions of the OPEIU in B.C. have led to a net loss in the number of organized bank workers.

In the long run, we do not think this kind of competition will be much more than a minor irritant. Because there are thousands of bank branches, each demanding time and patience on the part of union organizers, only a union like SORWUC which relies on the enthusiasm of volunteers can be successful in this field. SORWUC organizers are bank employees. As well, hundreds of women and men volunteer their time for leafletting and clerical and administrative work, because they are committed to the organization of women workers into a union controlled by women workers. We now have 600 members in six major chartered banks, with 14 branches certified and applications pending for 11 more. The number of bank employees who are educated in trade unionism and can answer anti-union arguments is growing rapidly.

We hope that the OPEIU's clumsy interference in bank organizing in B.C. will not stand in the way of improved relations between the CLC and ourselves. We hope that the approach of the Congress to organizing in the finance industry will be much more constructive. Again, we ask you to consider our urgent appeal for funds sent to you in July. We would be pleased to discuss this further, and suggest a meeting in Vancouver so that Congress officers could meet bank workers and other SORWUC members.
Yours sincerely,
Jean Rands
National President

Letter to Shirley Carr, Vice-President, CLC from SORWUC
October 6, 1977
Dear Sister Carr:

Enclosed please find a copy of a letter we are sending to unions in B.C. The response of bank workers to our organizing drive is excellent. Organizing is difficult, however, as bank workers are spread throughout the country in workplaces of five to thirty people. Since clerical workers in banks are over eighty per cent women, and our union was specifically formed to organize industries in which women are a majority, we are having considerable success in building a corps of dedicated, hardworking and knowledgeable women trade unionists.

The organizing campaign is expensive, and our small union of low-paid women workers can't possibly cover these costs from dues income. It is frustrating for us to have to spend so much time fund-raising, time which could more usefully be spent in organizing and education. It is especially frustrating when we know that the CLC has large sums of money set aside specifically for organizing office workers. As well as travel, printing and postage expenses associated with organizing, our small union has had to bear the expense of the precedent-setting CLRB decision, aspects of which are now being appealed by the banks to the federal court. We expect our legal expenses to be at least $15,000.

We wrote the CLC on July 5, requesting financial assistance. Although we have met and corresponded with representatives of the Congress, we have not yet had a reply to our request for funds. We feel that the organization of bank workers is important to the labour movement as a whole, and the CLC should support our campaign, regardless of the fact that we are not affiliated to the CLC. However, CLC representatives have indicated that affiliation is a stumbling block, and we therefore felt we should clarify our position. SORWUC is an independent union only because women workers here concluded that existing unions were not structured to meet the needs of women in the unorganized private sector, and that CLC affiliates had not taken on the task of organization in that area. While it would require a referendum for our union to join the CLC, our National Executive would be prepared to recommend that we affiliate if SORWUC could join as a national union with our own constitution and jurisdiction to organize the unorganized in all industries and occupations where women are a majority.

We view SORWUC not only as a union but as part of the movement for women's rights. This is not to say that we wish in any way to exclude or discriminate against men. Men are active and welcome in our union. But women workers should stand up for themselves. We believe that women should control the unions in which we are the majority. We are convinced that the main reason women clerical workers and service workers are hesitant to join unions is that existing unions are seen as another set of institutions dominated by men. SORWUC's success is due to the fact that our leaflets and bargaining demands deal directly with the specific problems of working women, and we are seen as an organization of working women organizing ourselves.

Our constitution may perhaps appear to be "ultra-democratic" but it is only through the widest practical dispersal of leadership functions that we can build a movement of women workers capable of organizing the private sector. All workers, including women, must develop pride and confidence in themselves in order to become effective trade unionists. We are attempting to build confidence and leadership skills among women workers. Since women workers have the administrative, technical and organizational skills that can be converted readily into the skills required for union leadership, we are in the happy position in which there need be little separation between members and full-time officials.

To date, the discussions we have had with CLC representatives have been cautious and tentative. A suggestion was made that SORWUC representatives meet in Ottawa with CLC officials. We would prefer that CLC officials come to Vancouver and meet with a larger number of our activists. This we feel would be the best way for the CLC to see that we are not just a small independent union, but actually the beginning of a mass movement of women workers.

We hope we can hear from you soon with a concrete offer of support for our organizing drive.

Yours sincerely,
Jean Rands
National President
Copies to B.C. Federation of Labour, CLC Women's Committee, B.C. Federation of Labour Women's Committee

Letter to SORWUC from Shirley Carr
November 1, 1977

Dear Ms. Rands:

This will acknowledge receipt of your correspondence dated October 6 and I regret the delay in replying. Before I am able to respond to all of your questions I will have to discuss this more fully with my fellow officers. Following this I shall be in touch with you again.

Yours sincerely,
Shirley G.E. Carr
Executive Vice-President

Letter to CLC from Saskatoon Bank Workers Organizing Committee
November 2, 1977

Dear Mr. Morris:

I am writing to you to raise very strong objections to the actions of one of your staff members Ray Sedgwick in Saskatoon.

I would also like to make a request for clarification of the CLC's policy on bank worker organizing as it relates to SORWUC.

As of the past few weeks Ray Sedgwick has involved himself with encouraging and assisting Mr. Terry Stevens of the Steelworkers to organize a Toronto Dominion Bank Branch in Saskatoon. He has continued to support the Steelworkers efforts to begin full time organizing in precisely the same bank branches which we are working with, and with the expressed intention of opposing SORWUC. He has also attempted (unsuccessfully) to remove the support which the Saskatoon Labour Council has given us for our organizing efforts.

The methods used by the Steelworkers and supported by Ray Sedgwick to obtain an application for certification in the TD branch have demonstrated opportunism, dishonesty, disregard for the rights of workers, and represented an overt act of provocation against the integrity of SORWUC.

We had been meeting with a group of workers from the TD Branch when Terry Stevens with Ray Sedgwick's backing decided to move in and sign up a number of the workers without informing us. Their methods of organizing included promising the women that they would bargain a contract for them. They attempted to brand our organization as incompetent; claimed that the information which we give to workers about the CLRB's regulations is incorrect; red baited our organization; and generally denied that we are organizing in Saskatchewan.

When we raised our objections to Ray Sedgwick his response was unacceptable to us. He stated that the CLC with his participation intended to actively oppose SORWUC from organizing, and would use whatever means necessary to sign up bank workers into an affiliate union. He refused to cooperate with us and stated that he fully supported the Steelworkers actions.

Stevens said that he had "CLC orders" to sign up bank workers; that Steel did *not* intend to represent the branch in bargaining; that he was getting involved mainly to prevent SORWUC from representing bank workers. Also the Steelworkers indicated that they will be hiring a full time bank organizer for Saskatoon.

I don't need to point out to you the nature of our objections to the actions and comments of these two men. Nor do I need to point out how their actions reflect on the reputation of the CLC at this time. Saskatchewan is a close community. There are many connections between workers in the thirty-seven bank branches in Saskatoon and the 300 branches in the province. The actions of this CLC affiliate union will have negative repercussions on the organizing efforts by both affiliates and non-affiliates. I'd like to point out that many affiliates have some trade union principles, support bank workers organizing, and abhor opportunistic

union fights which show total disregard for the rights and interests of workers.

We have developed a solid organization in Saskatchewan over the past months and are organizing in Saskatoon, Regina and a growing number of smaller centers in the province. We have direct support assistance from over thirty-six active women and men. Many of these organizers are trade unionists and are committed to assisting the unorganized women workers in this province. We intend to continue our work.

As you know the National Executive of SORWUC is interested to continue discussions with the CLC on the question of affiliation. At no point in these discussions, to my knowledge, have your representatives indicated that the CLC intends to actively oppose our organizing. It is my understanding that it would be best for all concerned if the organizing of bank workers was coordinated in such a way so as to avoid destructive competition. Our indications at the Saskatchewan level are that the actions of Ray Sedgwick and Terry Stevens are not in line with CLC direction on bank organizing.

What we would like to know is this: Do the actions of Ray Sedgwick represent the actual policy of the CLC on how to proceed with affiliate organizing of banks, and on how to relate to SORWUC?

As we are being brought into a public position on the Steelworkers actions in Saskatoon we require clarification of your executive's position on this matter quickly.

We are hopeful that this matter can be resolved.

Yours truly,

Jean Burgess

Coordinator, SORWUC Saskatchewan Copies to Shirley Carr; John McLeod, Sask. Federation of Labour; Jean Rands; Terry Stevens, Steelworkers; Ray Sedgwick, CLC.

Letter to UBW (Sask.) from CLC
November 16, 1977
Dear Ms. Burgess:

I am advised that you complained in regard to someone other than SORWUC being involved in organizing bank workers.

You may be assured that the CLC, in cooperation with its Federations, Labour Councils and affiliates, intends to help bank workers organize themselves so that they are a part of the Labour Movement in bargaining with the financial industry.

In that concern, the actions of Representatives Sedgwick and Stevens were in accord with the CLC's intentions and plans to organize bank workers into the CLC.

It may, on occasion, well occur that the above plans result in the CLC and its affiliates attempting to organize workers in which the organization you represent also has an interest. There is only one way in which those situations can be avoided and you have touched on it. In the interest of the welfare of bank workers, I would urge that SORWUC and/or its United Bank Workers join the CLC and together we will make common cause for the welfare of bank workers in Canada.

If there is an interest by the National Executive and membership of SORWUC and/or its United Bank Workers to meet again for the purpose of seriously discussing that objective, please feel free to contact me. I would be prepared to assist in convening such a meeting.

However, in the meantime we intend to organize bank workers so they are a part of the Canadian Labour Congress.

Yours truly,

E.W. Norheim

Regional Director of Organization, Prairie Provinces

Copies to: Joe Morris, Sask. Federation of Labour; R. Sedgwick; T. Stevens; Shirley Carr; Donald Montgomery; E. Johnston; T. Gooderham; Jean Rands.

(NOTE: Throughout the above letter, SORWUC was referred to as "SORWUK")

Letter to CLC from SORWUC
November 29, 1977

Dear Brother Morris,

We are enclosing a copy of our letter to you, dated October 6, 1977. Since we have not yet received an acknowledgement or reply, we are concerned that perhaps you did not receive the letter. We would also like to reiterate our desire for a meeting with CLC officials. We feel that it is important to meet before your National Executive meeting in December, so that both our union and your organization can clarify our respective positions.

We regret that we have not heard from you directly. Instead, our information has come solely through either rumour or the press. For instance, over a week ago, a Vancouver Sun reporter informed us that in an interview, Donald Montgomery had said among other things, "Negotiations with SORWUC are over;" 'That the CLC hoped that its affiliates would stop giving the United Bank Workers financial support'; and 'That SORWUC was insisting on sole jurisdiction rights for the banking industry as a condition of affiliation with the CLC.' This is not our position. Obviously some factual information has to be cleared up. We repeatedly tried to call Brother Montgomery last week before we responded to the reporter's questions, but our calls were not returned despite our messages that they were urgent.

We are also concerned about the fact that it has been almost two months now since your organization announced that it was co-ordinating a major bank organizing drive, and we cannot understand why the CLC has made no initiative to contact our union, which not only has gone on the record to say that it wishes to have serious discussions with the Congress regarding affiliation, but also at this point in time has 22 certifications in the banking industry and a current membership of almost 700 bank workers.

The second matter which we would like to discuss with you is the cost of the legal decision which allows unions, including your affiliates, to organize the banking industry. Obviously as you said in your last letter, the legal decision that extends bargaining rights to the employees of the banking industry is in a general sense the result of the battle that historically the trade union movement has won. However, specifically in terms of the branch by branch decision, our union is faced with a very concrete bill of $20,282.56 for fighting and winning that particular legal battle.

We have to date paid our lawyer, Ian Donald, the sum of $2500.00. Our union would like to ask the CLC to contribute the balance of the legal bill. If need be, you could send the money directly to our lawyer (Ian Donald, 195 Alexander St., Vancouver, B.C.) instead of sending the contribution through our union.

We look forward to hearing from you soon.

In Solidarity,
Jean Rands
National President
Copies to B.C. Federation of Labour, Vancouver & District Labour Council, CLC Vancouver Office, CLC Women's Committee, B.C. Federation of Labour Women's Committee.

Letter to the Executive of the CLC from SORWUC   December 7, 1977

SPECIAL DELIVERY
Brothers and Sisters:

Further to our letter of November 29, 1977, new developments have added urgency to our request for assistance in meeting legal costs.

The Royal Bank of Canada has announced that they will appeal the decision of the Canada Labour Relations Board allowing for branch by branch certification of banks. Should their appeal be successful, the result would be to overturn all certification in the banking industry.

Our small union is already faced with a legal bill of over $20,000 for the costs of the decisions which made it possible for your affiliates, as well as ourselves, to organize in the banking industry. It is no longer possible for us to undertake the financial responsibility for legal decisions that benefit the trade union movement as a whole.

As you know, our Union now holds 22 certifications in the banks. We have an organization of almost 700 bank employees and we are confident that bank employees will be organized, whatever the ground rules may be. We are not prepared to undertake further large expenses to defend the branch by branch decision in the federal court while you sit back and watch.

We feel the appeals to the federal court are a deliberate attempt by the banks to divert our resources from organizing to the courts. We regret that without substantial financial assistance from your organization, we will not be able to contest this appeal.

To reiterate our position regarding affiliation to the Congress, we wish to affiliate like any other national union. We are not asking for special treatment or special terms and conditions. Specifically, we are not asking for exclusive jurisdiction in the banking industry.

In solidarity,
Jean Rands
National President
Copies to B.C. Federation of Labour, Vancouver & District Labour Council, CLC Vancouver Office, CLC Women's Committee, B.C. Federation of Labour Women's Committee

Letter to SORWUC from CLC
December 14, 1977

Dear Sister Rands:

This will acknowledge receipt of your letter dated November 29th, 1977. I am sorry there was no reply to your correspondence of October 6th but it appeared a reply was unnecessary. That letter simply informed us of the determination of your union to reject any option other than the possible affiliation of SORWUC to the Congress if the Congress was prepared to provide your organization with substantial sums of money.

There were some allegations in your correspondence which we could take issue with, however, nothing would be gained by involving ourselves in writing on these issues. I must mention, however, the fact that the Office and Professional Employees International Union is an affiliate of the Congress and despite legislative and other impediments to organizing it has organized and has under collective agreement one hundred and thirty-nine establishments in the banking and credit institutions in Canada.

In your letter you state the Congress has made no initiative to contact your union. I should mention in this regard that there have been several contacts, the most recent when our Director of Organization accompanied by Brother Ken Rogers, the Secretary-Treasurer of the Canadian Union of Bankworkers and Laraine Singler of the BCGEU met with representatives from your organization to discuss the possibilities of the United Bank Workers becoming part of the national effort on behalf of bank employees. There was no follow-up to that meeting because the impression they received was that while your organization desperately needed the finances and experienced personnel to deal with collective bargaining in this specialized field, your organization was not prepared to make the necessary arrangements, and indeed, continued to cling to the conviction that your union could take on the banking industry.

It is our firm conviction that the job to be done on behalf of bank-workers, i.e. organization, negotiation, servicing and the educational and research roles will require the total resources of the movement; and that while small independent groups will make some individual progress, it has been our experience that in the long term the lack of a strong and well organized movement to deal with the strongly entrenched banking industry could be detrimental to the best interests of the workers involved. History is replete with examples of this.

In conclusion then, let me state, it is in the best interests of the United Bank Workers to join the movement to establish a Canadian Union of Bank Workers and an application by the United Bank Workers to accomplish this would be welcomed by the Congress and facilitated with dispatch.

You will understand that any consideration of SORWUC's position within the Congress structure would require a detailed examination of the units involved in relation to the question of jurisdiction granted to affiliates of the Congress, however, the immediate and more pressing issue is to protect the interests of bank workers and to build an organization representative of their needs and desires. To this end the Executive Council would consider an application from the United Bank Workers to become a part of the proposed national structure. If this were to happen we would be prepared to look at the financial obligations outstanding in connection

with the applications for certification of United Bank Worker units.

Hoping to hear from you on this matter, I remain,
Fraternally yours,
Joe Morris,
President
Copies to D. Montomery (Secretary/Treasurer, CLC; E. Johnston (Director of Organization,CLC); B.C. Federation of Labour; Vancouver & District Labour Council; CLC Vancouver Office; CLC Women's Committee; B.C. Federation of Labour Women's Committee

Letter to CLC from Charlotte Johnson, UBW   January 17, 1978

Dear Mr. Morris:
Re: Your letter of December 14, 1977 to J. Rands, National President of S.O.R.W.U.C.
The above letter was discussed at the United Bank Workers Section Executive meeting of January 8, 1978. Your suggestion that the UBW Section of SORWUC split from SORWUC and apply independently for affiliation to the CLC was rejected unanimously by our Executive.

We find it reprehensible on your part that you would suggest we should divide our Union in order to affiliate to the Congress. Your letter states that SORWUC's jurisdiction is too broad and therefore a hindrance to Congress affiliation. Yet, the USWA, a Congress affiliate, has applied to the CLRB to represent bank employees in Saskatchewan.

To date the actions of your organization have only confused bank employees and caused problems in organizing.

Let us reiterate that SORWUC would be prepared to affiliate to the CLC as a National Union. If your Executive is unwilling to consider this request we see no purpose in continuing correspondence.
Sincerely,
C. Johnson, President
United Bankworkers Section of SORWUC
Copies to S. Carr; L. Singler; B.C. Federation of Labour; Saskatchwan Federation of Labour; Vancouver & District Labour Council; Women's Committee, B.C. Federation of Labour

Letter to UBW from CLC
January 31, 1978

Dear Sister Johnson:

This will acknowledge receipt of your correspondence dated Tuesday, January 17th, 1978 in which you state your Executive have unanimously rejected the concept of the United Bankworkers affiliation with the Canadian Labour Congress, and as well, that you see no purpose in continuing correspondence.

While it would appear from the wording of your constitution, that such an important decision would be made by the members, after a thorough discussion of the pros and cons of affiliation, the tremendous job of building a Canadian Union of Bank Employees, and the viability of S.O.R.W.U.C., we have no intention of appealing the decision made by your Executive on behalf of bankworkers.

We will respect the decision of your Executive and cease all correspondence on the subject.

Fraternally yours,
Joe Morris,
President;
Copies to D. Montogmery; S. Carr; L. Singler; B.C. Federation of Labour; Saskatchewan Federation of Labour; Vancouver & District Labour Council; Women's Committee—B.C. Federation of Labour; T. Gooderham; W. Norheim

Glossary

Affiliate: Unions that are members (and have voting privileges) of a larger body of labour.

Application for Certification: where a union has at least 35% of the employees in an appropriate bargaining unit or workplace as members in good standing, application is made to the Labour Relations Board to be certified to represent these employees for the purposes of collective bargaining.

Association of University & College Employees: an independent democratic union representing workers at Simon Fraser University, The University of B.C., Capilano College, New Caledonia College and the teaching assistants at Simon Fraser University. AUCE was formed in 1972 by UBC clerical workers, 95% of whom were women. Often referred to as SORWUC's sister union.

Bargaining Agent: union designated by a Labour Relations Board as the exclusive representative of all employees in a bargaining unit for the purposes of negotiations with the employer.

Bargaining Unit: group of workers deemed by the Labour Relations Board as having sufficient interests in common that all these interests can be served by one collective agreement, negotiated by one bargaining agent.

Canada Labour Code: see labour code.

Board: see Canada Labour Relations Board.

Canadian Labour Congress: an organization consisting of the Canadian sections of unions which are affiliated to the AFL-CIO in the U.S., plus large Canadian unions like the Canadian Union of Public Employees and the Canadian Brotherhood of Railway, Transport & General Workers, and government employees' organizations. A union must be affiliated to the CLC in order to affiliate to provincial federations of labour and local labour councils.

Canada Labour Relations Board: established under the Canada Labour Code to administer labour law, including certification of trade unions as bargaining agents, investigation of unfair labour practices and other functions prescribed under the legislation.

Caucus Meetings: take place when one party wishes to leave the room to privately discuss an issue. The decision or position taken is then reported back to the other party. Caucus meetings are common during negotiations.

Certification: official designation by a labour relations board of a union as sole and exclusive bargaining agent for employees in a bargaining unit. Following certification the employer is required to recognize the union and make a reasonable effort to sign a union contract.

Collective Agreement: a contract between a union acting as bargaining agent, and an employer covering wages, hours, working conditions, fringe benefits, rights of workers and union, and procedures to be followed in settling disputes and grievances. Also referred to as a contract, union contract, or agreement.

Collective Bargaining: method of determining wages, hours and other conditions of employment through direct negotiations between the union and the employer.

Normally, the result of collective bargaining is a written contract which covers all employees in the bargaining unit. Strikes and lock-outs are an accepted part of the collective bargaining process.

Conciliation: third party intervention by a conciliation officer (an employee of the Department of Labour) to assist with negotiations. If a conciliation officer is unsuccessful in helping the parties settle a contract, he reports to the Minister of Labour, who then either: a) agrees that the parties are to be left to settle the dispute through economic pressure i.e. strike or lock-out, or, b) appoints a Conciliation Commission or a Conciliation Board (independent of the Department of Labour). The Commission or Board then study the positions of both sides and ordinarily make a public report, which is not binding on either party.

Federation of Labour: a provincial federation of local unions and labour councils chartered by the Canadian Labour Congress.

Grievance: complaint against management by one or more employees concerning an alleged injustice, or, where a contract exists, an alleged breach of the union contract. Procedures for handling grievances are defined in the contract.

Hearing(s): a procedure whereby a Board or Court call the parties to appear in person to present evidence to demonstrate facts, and argument as to the interpretation of the law. In the case of the CLRB the hearings are usually conducted by a panel of three Board members.

Initiation Fee: specific amount of money paid by a new member to a union upon joining. The payment of an initiation fee is an essential part of the evidence required by the Board to prove membership in the union.

Investigating Officer: employee of the CLRB who does preliminary investigations on applications for certification (checking union membership records and their authenticity, and cross-checking these with the employer's payroll, etc.), and unfair labour practice complaints.

Labour Code: legislation that is passed by a Provincial or Federal parliament setting basic ground rules and standards of conduct for industrial relations i.e. how does a union become certified, what constitutes an unfair labour practice complaint, how and when can a union strike, etc.

Labour Council: organization composed of local unions in a given community or district chartered by the CLC.

Local Union: the basic unit of union organization. Trade unions are usually divided into a number of locals for the purposes of local administration. Locals have their own by-laws and usually elect their own officers.

National Union: (SORWUC) meets annually in Convention. The body of the union that basically consists of an executive and is responsible for certifications throughout Canada, where no local union exists. The National union finances are made up of per capita dues (one half of the local union dues, not to exceed $3.00) from Locals and Sections. Every member of SORWUC (Local 1, Local 3 and the UBW Section) is a member of the National union. The SORWUC bank certifications were held by the National union. The executive is elected annually by referendum.

Negotiations: the process where the union negotiating committee and management representatives meet to discuss contract proposals and hopefully, reach agreement by compromise. The parties should eventually reach agreement and sign the union contract governing wages and working conditions which is then binding on both management and the union, after ratification by the union membership.

Organizing Committee: a group of UBW members in a particular geographic area that co-ordinate the organizing drive i.e. elect its own executive, leaflet, meet, present statements to the press, etc. An organizing committee functions like a local.

Raid: when a group of unionized employees decide they wish to be represented by another union, the second union is said to be "raiding" the first. Where a union contract exists, raids can only take place during the 7th and 8th month of the contract.

Referendum Ballot: a manner of conducting a vote where a ballot is mailed to each member and is then returned to the union office by a set date when all ballots are to be counted. This is done to ensure that all members cast a vote on important issues (contract proposals, a change in union policy, election of officers etc.), whether or not they attend meetings.

Representation Vote: a vote conducted by the Labour Relations Board to determine whether a majority of employees in a bargaining unit wish union representation. If a majority of those voting are in favour of the union, the union will be certified.

Seniority: term used to designate an employee's status relative to other employees as in determining order of layoff, promotion, recall, transfer, vacation etc. Depending on the provision of the union contract, seniority is ordinarily based on length of continuous or interrupted service. Seniority can be based on length of service with a company, a department, a branch, or an industry.

Steward: a person elected by the people that she/he works with as their union representative. Where a collective agreement exists, the steward is responsible for ensuring that it is enforced and representing employees in grievances vs. management. Where no contract exists, the steward is responsible for communications to and from the union office, keeping the morale up, and being the spokesperson in anti-union arguments with management.

Scab: or strikebreaker, usually refers to individuals hired to perform the work of employees who are on strike. The term is also applied to any person crossing a picket line.

Strike: a cessation of work or a refusal to work or to continue to work by employees, following a secret ballot vote to do so, for the purpose of compelling an employer to agree to terms or conditions of employment. Usually the last stage of collective bargaining, when all other means have failed.

Trade Union: voluntary association or organization of workers to further their mutual interests with respect to wages, hours of work, working conditions, recognition and respect, and other matters of interest to workers.

Union Dues: an amount of money given to the union on a monthly basis, to help pay for the day to day operation of the union.

Union Security: provisions in a union contract designed to protect the life of the union at the workplace i.e. where every worker covered by the contract must become or remain a member of the union. New workers need not be union members to be hired, but must join after a certain number of days, or hours worked. Also covers dues, check-off and membership requirements i.e. closed shop, union shop, modified union shop, rand formula, and open shop.

Section (SORWUC): members of organizing committees, local and headquarters members who work in a common industry i.e. UBW Section and UBW Saskatchewan Section. Elects its own executive and has its own by-laws.

Unfair Labour Practice Complaint: a charge that management has failed to abide by the laws as set out in the labour code. The Labour Board receives written submission from union and management. An IRO investigator attempts settlement. If the complaint is not settled, the Board will usually order a hearing to hear evidence before ruling whether or not an unfair labour practice has occurred.

Working Conditions: conditions pertaining to the workers' job environment such as hours of work, safety, rest periods, uniforms, machinery, renovations, wickets, etc. Usually included in, and subject to the union contract.

Press Gang is a feminist printing and publishing collective which was established in the spring of 1974. Since then, we have been working in the printed media to produce all kinds of books, posters, pamphlets and leaflets. Our interests are in printed materials that critically examine the role of women in Canada. We want to produce work that fights the sexual stereotypes that oppress us and our children. We want to explore ourselves as women in a sexist society, and to make it clear why we need to change our social, political, and economic conditions.

Other titles by Press Gang:
Fishermarket and Other Poems
Women Look at Psychiatry
Jody Said
Muktu: the Backward Muskox
The Anti-Psychiatry Bibliography and Resource Guide

Press Gang Publishers
603 Powell Street
Vancouver, B.C. V6A 1H2
(604) 253-1224